A SOPHISTICATED
FORM OF
HAWK WATCHING

KENN FILKINS

They will
mount up on wings
like eagles. . .

Isaiah 40:31 (NASB)

A SOPHISTICATED FORM OF
HAWK WATCHING

A Collection of Falconry Stories

KENN FILKINS

BAYWING HAWK PRESS

SAULT STE. MARIE, MICHIGAN

A Sophisticated Form of Hawk Watching

First Edition

Cover Photo of "Sadie" taken by Marti Filkins.

All photos and illustrations by the author,
unless otherwise noted.

Address all correspondence to:

Baywing Hawk Press
533 Maple St.
Sault Ste. Marie, MI 49783
E-mail: kennf@charter.net
Web site: www.filkinsfoto.com

Dedication

*To God, the Creator,
and my Savior Jesus,
for making this wonderful
world with hawks, falcons
and eagles.*

Other books
by
Kenn Filkins

Comfort Those Who Mourn:
How to Preach Personalized Funeral Messages

Fly Fishing for Salmon & Steelhead of the Great Lakes

A Comforting Word

Seven Sayings One Friday

Seven Sayings:
The Impact of Jesus' Sayings from
the Cross (Kindle eBook)

Characters of Calvary

Preaching Personalized Funerals
In a Digital Age

Fine Day for Squirrels (Kindle eBook)

and edited by Kenn Filkins
A Bond with the Wild:
A Celebration of American Falconry.

*For ordering information contact Kenn Filkins
at Baywing Hawk Press or search Amazon.com,
Amazon's Kindle E-books and
CreateSpace.com for a hard copy of this book.*

Introduction

Falconry is the most sophisticated form of bird watching.

This Sport of Kings uniquely offers falconers a chance to see hawks, falcons and eagles do what they were created to do — chase wild quarry. Additionally, falconers do more than simply observe hawks hunting; they actively participate in the adventures.

Those adventures and the bonds formed with the birds of prey prompted this book.

A Sophisticated Form of Hawk Watching is a collection of falconry stories showing many aspects of how falconers practice this ancient sport in the modern age.

These stories cover a broad spectrum of experiences and emotions falconers encounter in this sport: Joy, excitement, fear, pain, satisfaction, anticipation, relief, laughter and love all flow from our relationships with these wonderful creatures.

The 25 chapters share stories of young love, sheer bravery, companionship, loss, jackrabbit hawking, dog attacks, hawk trapping, field meets, dilemmas, conservation and much more.

Some historical firsts are detailed too including: the invention of car-hawking, and the creation of removable anklets — that are now used around the world and featured in most falconry supply catalogs.

Unique raptor writings also appear in these pages such as: a historical fiction piece of Genghis Khan hunting with golden eagles, spring raptor trapping and banding at Whitefish Point, a history-making rescue of a bald eagle with West Nile Virus and several zany dog stories in "Terrier Dreams."

Other notable stories include:

• "A Falconry Parable," sharing humorous insights into all "species" of falconers,

• The fun "Jackrabbit Rescue," story showing a falconer's respect and compassion for prey,

• "On Wings Like Eagles," presenting Isaiah 40:31 from a falconer's unique viewpoint,

• "Dialogue 101," detailing an interesting conversation with a not-so-casual onlooker,

• "Hoodwinking," displaying a humorous take on hood-making, and

• "Animal Rights — Christian Morals," tackling a presumed conflict between Christian principles and hunting.

Some of the chapters are updated from previously published articles and many stories are new works, such as "Fine Weather for Squirrels."

These stories give you the inside look at a falconer's joys, trials and adventures.

Enjoy the journey.

Table of Contents

Introduction

Sarah's first season, with the author, a cottontail and Prince, the rat terrier pup, pause for a photo near the cemetery in Rolling Prairie, Indiana in 1982.

Chapter 1
Young Love:
Sarah's First Season

On Tuesday June 22, 1982, at 10:17 a.m. at the Chicago O'Hare International Airport, I met the lady who would become my mistress.

Her name was Sarah Kedar.

She had a tall, lean athletic build with big, yellow feet. She was a Harris hawk chick.

"Sarah Kedar" is Hebrew for "Lady in Black." For me the underlying implication was "Mistress of Death."

By the 4th of July, she was hard-penned and near her flying weight of 32 ounces (907 grams).

During her first season she chased anything in sight. One time she rolled a woodchuck head over heels. After it tumbled, the chuck stood up on its hind feet with the nimbleness of a gymnast — as if the whole maneuver was planned. After the first strike, Sarah took a stand in a four-foot-high bush and turned to look at him. The woodchuck let out a loud war cry and prepared to fight her. It pleased me that she didn't take it up on the offer as I quickly interceded. She would also push home the attack on muskrats while *I* was duck hunting, at times she even entered the water in pursuit.

Another time while rabbit hawking, I kicked up several bunnies from one small area — a rare but happy occasion — but I didn't see a flight at the fleeing cottontails.

She must have caught a bunny trying to escape out the other side, I thought. Expectantly, I ran over to find Sarah and my terrier Prince working side by side. Prince was digging up a nest of meadow voles and grabbing them one by one and flipping them aside. Sarah collected the castoffs and promptly deposited them in her crop. Ringnecked pheasants were also on her list of catchable quarry. She feathered ten or twelve of the few we saw. Only one came home for supper.

Sarah never did grab a cat even with several chances, and obviously this pleased me. But dogs, I'm sad to say, were a different story. Snakes and a wide assortment of birds were also on her bill of fare.

At dawn one day we worked near a woodlot next to a feral field in town. We sought some early morning bunnies. I knew crows roosted nightly in these woods, but I didn't give them much thought after I heard them leave at first light. Sarah was seven feet up in a tree on my right and about 10 feet away. As I walked by her, she flew over me and bolted off to the left. As she flew by, I searched to see a bunny I thought I'd missed. When I turned I didn't see a bunny, I saw a crow 40 feet away that had just dropped to feed on the ground. It flew straight up and was 10 to 12 feet up when Sarah pitched up and slammed into it. That was her second crow kill of the year. She also feathered several other crows, one of which she tagged a chase to the top of a 45-foot phone pole.

Hawking with a Dog

Another added dimension to Sarah's first year was the addition, on December 16, of a 16-week-old terrier to our hawking team. Prince was my Christmas present. Each day I worked to introduce Prince to the team. I flew Sarah in the yard with the dog on a leash to keep him close enough to ward off an assault by her.

She soon began to "accept" the dog and would even fly past him as they both chased the lure. Yes, I trained the dog to the lure too. It was heartening at that time to have Sarah grab the lure instead of the dog.

Prince was born to hunt. He came from good working stock from an old German immigrant's game farm. He was larger than the maximum size recommended in the article on mini-dogs (see August '82 *Hawk Chalk*, pp. 46-47). On Christmas Day '82, while my two young sons were enjoying a holiday nap, I went hawking in a nearby field. It was a training exercise more than a hardcore hunt. Sarah grabbed the pup every time he wandered more than six feet from me. At the time, I wondered if all I had done was create a new method to train a dog to work close. Sarah caught him three times. When the hunt's only bunny flushed, she took it with real style with Prince running close behind. Sarah was gorged on her holiday meal and Prince was also fed some warm rabbit meat. Thus began a happy and serviceable companionship. Prince was tied near the weathering area when he was not in the house. The following summer they sat side by side for hours and played. The terrier would put his paw into the weathering area and Sarah would fly down and nip — but not bite — him on the nose, ear or butt. That was a delightful sight, but let any other dog come near and. . . .

In January of her first season, in a large Indiana city, we worked a bunny field that was filled with mounds of briars. I casually pointed out some fox prints in the snow to my friend as we walked into the area. I assumed the prints were from the night before. We soon kicked up a cottontail that ran down a snow-covered path into the biggest briar patch. I had hoped that young Prince had learned the game and would pursue the fleeing bunny then flush it from the cover. He did not chase it. Conversely, as we got closer to the patch, he began to sniff the air, walked stiff-legged with his hackles raised and barked ferociously. I had never seen such a display from him. It looked like an odd mixture of fear and aggression.

"Oh great," I said to my friend. "He's afraid of rabbits."

Just then he bolted into the briars and Sarah stooped into the center of the patch, which was much too thick to penetrate. She then flew straight up and stooped again while the quarry was still in the brush. For a moment she was hung up on briars. Then I got a cursory glance at a red streak disappearing into an adjacent woods. Prince had bolted a red fox and Sarah tried to put the clamps on it.

Cottontails: Sarah's Favorite

With all of Sarah's attempts at miscellaneous quarry, her favorite was cottontail. One winter flight was at an abandoned drive-in theater when the temperature hovered around zero. A friend and I were working some cover near a metal fence. Prince bolted a cottontail, which made some nifty moves, then dipped under the fence and disappeared into one of the grass-covered parking slants. Sarah took her stand on the projection booth while we sought the hidden treasure.

After the fruitless search, we headed back to the adjacent field. Halfway back we flushed the rabbit, which ran between us and directly toward Sarah. Sarah flew head-on toward the rabbit, but at the last instant it made a 90-degree turn and was quickly making its escape up over each parking slant. The bunny barely seemed to lose speed with the sharp turn, but Sarah came completely to grips with inertia. She leaped up quickly after her miss and overhauled the cottontail from a standstill. Its running start was not enough to save it from her talons. She pulled the same flight on another occasion when my brothers and I were hawking, only that time she caught the bunny in a shorter distance.

Another flight characteristic she showed her first season was the "yo-yo" flight. The field was well-worn from winter's beating and the brush was low. Sarah was following close and sat in a group of short trees. The rabbit flushed and ran down a footpath. She flew up on a incline until she was over the bunny. Sarah then stooped and footed the rabbit, but poorly so. As the cottontail quickly shot off to the right down a smaller trail, Sarah flew up over the quarry 20-25 feet and stooped again. She made four such yo-yo stoops before the rabbit reached the tree line 100 yards away.

She was stationed high in a tree when I re-flushed the bunny. It ran directly under Sarah who promptly snagged it. She was really getting kicked around, which was unusual for her, especially since she had a head hold on it. This was absolutely the biggest wild cottontail I had ever seen. It was at least twice the size of a normal cottontail. To top the flight off, the rabbit bit her on the bottom of the foot. Really, it did. The mega-bunny got away just as I reached her to lend a hand, so, unfortunately, no photos were taken to confirm its immense size.

One-Day Hawking Meet

Sarah's love for the hunt was shown the last Saturday in January when some northern Indiana falconers gathered for a one-day hawk-ing meet. We drove several miles to an industrial area. Sunny skies, a gentle breeze and 20-degree weather greeted us as the Harris hawks — including Sarah and her brother, flown by Ted Nusbaum, of Osceola, Indiana — were flown first. The siblings were up in a small tree when we bolted the first bunny only 20 feet into the field. The rabbit was caught in an excited flurry of black feathers, ringing bells, brown fur and yellow feet. Both hawks were on him so fast it was impossible to tell just which one nabbed it first. Either would have caught it alone. After that we had several flights including a 120-yard, shifting Harris hawk tail-chase that ended with both hawks slamming into the rabbit simultaneously — inches from a warren. Both hawks were once again rewarded as they easily traded off the quarry. Ted fed-up his tiercel Harris for its successful day. Sarah flew free as we tramped back to the vehicles to get the other birds. On the walk, she caught her first solo rabbit of the day. After yet another reward, her crop was bulging.

The red-tailed hawks then took their turns. One red-tail scored quickly and with great style. The passage male was gorged up. The other red-tail's weight was a bit too high and acted accordingly. With the male Harris and one red-tail done for the day, only a non-respon-sive red-tail was left for hunting.

Someone asked if Sarah would still hunt.

"We can try, but I'm not making any promises," I said.

Sarah looked off balance and front heavy with her huge crop. But she responded fine and her next kill came after a long and successful chase. The rabbit had already made it to cover when Sarah plunged in and the squeal sounded.

"That is it for her," I said, more to myself than to anyone else.

Soon, she was completely, fully, absolutely, totally gorged!

As we walked back across of the field, we kept flushing rabbits. The cottontails flushed from cover, ran left to right across the field to some mowed grass then back past us to the area we had just hawked. From the fist, Sarah stared hard at each of the fleeing critters but never bated. Finally, a falconer, 70 yards ahead of us, flushed a bunny that did the same maneuver but ran directly toward us. It stopped half-way between the falconer and us.

They were all yelling when I said, "Let my puppy chase it!"

Just then the bunny took off again. The five-month-old terrier bolted after it.

In all the excitement, someone screamed, "Release the hawk."

Inexplicability, I obeyed, lifting my arm.

Instantly, Sarah was off and after one quick wingover, the rabbit was done.

She then gave me an odd look, as to say, "Well, now what? I can't swallow one more bite!"

She could not accept any reward, so she nonchalantly stepped onto my glove and surrendered her prize.

Brother, Sister Act

Ted and I often hunted Sarah and her brother together their first season. She would not crowd in on his kills. She would land a few feet away then look intently at him, as if to say, "I'm here if you need any help." Unfortunately, we got to see what would happen when the quarry broke free. She flew it down and recaptured it.

Obviously, Sarah is not the best game hawk or even the best Harris hawk, nor did we have the best season that year. But we had a great time — even without a huge head count.

But, when you're in love, you want to tell someone — everyone! I love Harris hawks. . . .

Most of all, I love my Lady in Black!

PHOTO BY DEBBIE GRIFFITH

Raider with a fox squirrel she caught on the farm of Dr. Larry Smith DVM in Rolling Prairie, Indiana.

Chapter 2
Raider of the Lost Squirrel

At the first mention of squirrels we conjure up images of those playful creatures we see here in the Midwest. One June Sunday as I walked to church a familiar sound caught my attention. Two fox squirrels ran down the trunk of a big oak tree in the church yard.

One squirrel was much larger than the other. A mother and a wayward youngster, I assumed. The mother was either chasing it into or away from the nest. Their antics seemed playful and the youngster appeared so successful at evasion that I couldn't tell which the mom doing. Up, down and around they darted. The youngster always won. Seeing me close by didn't startle them. Apparently squirrels can see the difference between a Bible and a red-tailed hawk.

An example of a squirrel's evasiveness happened that morning. During one escape the youngster shot quickly out along a secondary limb that stretched toward a neighboring tree. That branch was bark free so the youngster slipped and almost fell. By the time it had regained its footing the mom was running full-bore on the branch toward it.

"She has him now!" I said. To my surprise, the youngster ran straight toward its charging mom. Just as they were to collide, the son dropped under the limb and kept running full-tilt to make yet another escape. The mom stopped in sheer amazement and looked over her shoulder. She gave up the chase as he calmly scampered down the tree and across the lawn to yelp at the hawks in the weathering area.

Climbing Demons

These extremely playful creatures are not the same ones we encounter in the woodlots of Indiana. They may look the same and even use the same tree or nest hole, but they are not the same.

In historic English fables, authors exaggerated the prowess and ferocity of the hero's enemy. This exaggeration exalted the hero to supreme heights for conquering such a fiendish foe. There is, however, no need for such exaggeration when speaking of the prowess and ferocity of the squirrels we hunt. When attacked by a hawk, squirrels bite, kick, scratch, fight, gnaw and in general are not very submissive.

In northern Indiana, my a female red-tailed hawk flew at fox squirrels — the largest and heaviest North American squirrel species (Sciurus niger). In small towns like Rolling Prairie the popular red-tail hunting spots, such as industrial lots, were not within daily reach. The most common prey for practical hawking was not rabbits but squirrels.

Raider

My female red-tail "Raider" chased squirrels with a natural vigor. On December 27, when she was trapped, I found a bite on her upper right thigh marked with dried blood. I assumed she hunting squirrels while wintering in northern Indiana. Later hunting experiences confirmed that suspicion.

In our area, fox squirrels inhabit the groves of timbers — oak islands — with very little ground cover between the trees. As a result we found fox squirrels in cow pastures where only the big oaks offered protection, Raider made most of her kills on the ground and made an all-out effort to catch any squirrel that touched the ground.

Grey squirrels are most active in the early morning and late evening, and it seems fox squirrels rise later and are more active during mid-day. From 9 a.m. to noon was a great time to hawk the fox. At that time squirrels were not only active but searching for food on the ground.

The fox squirrels tend not to hoard food but rather to put on thick layers of fat when food is plentiful. These layers of fat must be replenished throughout the winter.

Even though Raider hunted squirrel naturally, I had apprehension about flying her at the climbers. One squirrel bite can cripple a bird for life and penetrating its hide is difficult. Its razor-sharp nails are used to strike at the hawk or even scratch her eyes. Falconers in my circumstance are faced with a "lesser of these evils" decision.

I asked myself, "Should I let my hawk vegetate and go hawking only when there's time to drive to a bunny field? Or shall I go hawking often in my neighborhood and hunt squirrels with the inherent dangers?"

The choice is obvious, but difficult.

For all of its problems, squirrel hawking provides very exciting flights. The chases are highly visual and often create long-lasting flights with plenty of cunning and maneuvering by both predator and prey. On one hunt Raider made a pass at a two-pound fox squirrel and pushed it into a vulnerable position. The squirrel seemed trapped in a 30-foot-tall stump, a foot and a half in diameter with very few branches and no holes. Raider watched from high in a nearby tree as I beat the trunk from below. The squirrel knew its disadvantage but he didn't give up.

Raider made a couple passes then bound to him on the top of the stump. She didn't have a good hold and it quickly bit her. She released it to get another hold, but it darted down the side. It then screamed its war cry, but not that noisy chatter that red squirrels make: It belched a deep, raspy, almost demonic cry. It sounded like a curse.

After several more passes, the squirrel made a quick and bold leap for a thickly branched tree while Raider was a little out of position. She chased him up and down it for several minutes to no avail. She then flew off 50 yards. Raider wouldn't come back even when I shouted the escape signal, as the squirrel ran from tree to tree and finally to a nest. Raider was bitten far too often during her first season. However, my journal revealed she never went home without a squirrel on any day one bit her. Squirrel bites can be very infectious, so I treat all bites in the field with antibiotic cream. Raider's first season was long before falconers invented "squirrel chaps" to protect them from the dangerous bites.

Tools for Squirrel Hawking

In the woodlots, a hawking tool was made from anything that was not tied down. Items such as sticks, stones, logs and even snow balls were used to flush hiding prey. More than once our beating sticks have become not only useful but necessary tools.

Once Raider pursued a fox squirrel so hard through a very thick woods that it tried to hide in a broken tree stump. When it climbed inside this opening, I used my beating stick to pin it to the inside wall of the trunk. I pulled almost all the fur off its tail getting it out of the tree.

A more common incident occurs when the stick is thrown at a squirrel to keep it moving from tree to tree, branch to branch or on the ground. On one occasion a squirrel was running on the snow, so I yelled the escape signal and threw my stick at the squirrel. Tossing the stick seems to confuse the squirrel and to draw the attention of the hawk. Raider footed the squirrel in the snow and was promptly bitten.

She released it, then for a few milliseconds, they sat on the snow a few feet apart. Then like a flash of lightning, Raider used one wing beat and a swift left jab to end the hunt. After her crop was full, we started for the van but I could not find my favorite flushing stick. I dug through the snow and searched the area several times while re-enacting the flight. It was all to no avail until I looked up. The stick hung horizontally six feet up in a tree and 20 feet from the squirrel's path. At least the toss was in the right direction! Obviously, the toss had no impact on the catch.

Toward the Horizon

Raider demonstrated her talent for squirrel hawking one afternoon when she caught her first squirrel with me. She had killed a cottontail on her first free flight a few days earlier. This day we worked a fence line between a cemetery near an old hardwood lot. Raider spotted something in the middle of the oaks and took chase. She targeted a fox squirrel digging for food in the snow. It scrambled to escape as the hawk chased it up a tree. She almost grabbed the squirrel as it disappeared into a large, high, leaf nest.

"That's it for that squirrel," I informed my new red-tail. "Let's look for another."

Then she looked toward the horizon.

I had seen that look before.

And it scared me.

I had seen that identical look from another recently captured red-tailed hawk at an Indiana Falconers' Association meet in South Bend. That day, a large crowd of onlookers gathered in a popular rabbit field as the falconer unhooded a beautiful and unique albino red-tailed hawk. The presence of this hawk created much excitement at the state field meet. The white hawk seemed ill at ease. Maybe it was the crowd, the unfamiliar hunting field or its weight. But something seemed amiss.

"Don't turn that hawk loose," I softly said to the falconer. "You don't have to fly her now. Maybe she is spooked by all the people or is a touch high in weight."

But the peer pressure and the excitement were overwhelming and he released her. She flew right to the top of a leafless tree. Others started to beat the brush, but I watched her.

Then she looked off into the horizon.

"Call her down," I begged the falconer. "She looks ready to leave."

She looked back. He paused.

She stared off into the distance again.

He started calling her down.

She glanced at him, then turned away.

She flew into the wind. Away from us. She carried no telemetry transmitter.

We looked for hours and hours.

She was never seen again.

When I saw my recently trapped red-tail give that same look, I panicked and instantly began calling her down.

As I waved the lure, she glanced at me, then looked to the horizon again.

The passager looked intently at the leaf nest in towering oak, then ignoring me, she flew above the tree tops upwind of the nest.

Away from me.

I panicked.

I screamed, blew the whistle and swung the lure.

All to no avail.

She just flew off into the wind.

As she flew, Raider climbed into the wind above the tree canopy. When she was 60 feet from the nest she spread her wings and tail fully then tilted straight up. The stiff wind shoved her like a gale against a sail. She shot her back toward the nest. With the added speed from the wind she charged full-bore into the nest. The smash created a resounding thump. Sticks and leaves flew in every direction as the bewildered squirrel was forcibly ejected from its home.

The stunned squirrel regained its wits enough to make a second escape to yet another nest. Its second shelter was built on a large stick nest. It was safe.

After that flight she was named Raider, for her plundering of the nest.

The Scrap

Later that afternoon Raider chased a fox squirrel that ran from a bush toward an oak. The red-tail caught up to it at the bottom of the tree. The squirrel ran around the base and planned to climb the back side, but Raider made a sweeping pass around the trunk and scraped it off the trunk.

Raider evicted another squirrel from a leaf nest later in the season, but she paid no attention to leaf nests unless she saw a squirrel disappear into it.

This dangerous quarry provided accessible and enjoyable hunting adventures for hawks with the moxie to challenge them. It also reminded us that falconers are more than observers; we are partners and intimate observers of the often long battles with memories that seem immortal.

Sarah and Shogun II share a perch for a photo op in Rolling Prairie, Indiana.

Chapter 3
A Cast of Harris Hawks

For me the lure of falconry was always building relationships with the raptors.

That bond and hunting opportunities allows me to see their God-given talent. Decades ago I saw a pencil sketch in a wildlife magazine that depicted a pair of red-tailed hawks flying in a cast at a fox squirrel. That sketch burned in my soul one aspect that I consider the ultimate falconry experience. From that day I desired to hunt a pair of hawks in a cast in the fall and winter, breed them in the spring, and raise their young in the summer.

The Harris hawks' genetics and social nature make this possible for falconers.

Harris hawks are the adaptable, gregarious desert birds that, through captive breeding, have been extending their falconry habitat north and around the world. While enjoying some degree of success, there are some inherent problems with flying a species originating from the hot, arid, desert country in the cold, humid, sometimes frozen country of northern Indiana.

The Season

During the 1983-84 season I flew a cast of Harris hawks that were hunted and housed together. The female Harris, Sarah, was in her second season. She was bred by Steve Heying of Ashland, Missouri. The tiercel, "Shogun II," in his first season, was bred by Tom Coulson of Louisiana. Sarah flew between 32 and 39 ounces (907-1105 grams), while the tiercel flew between 24 and 27 ounces (680-765 grams).

The Best Of Both Worlds

Cast flights seemed like a combination of competition and cooperation between the hawks. It was often impossible to tell if they were competing for the game or cooperating to catch it, yet they never crabbed over a kill and would receive their gorge on opposite ends of the same rabbit.

Flying a cast of a female and tiercel Harris was the best of both worlds. Sarah never liked fist flights and always sought out an elevated perch.

Shogun, on the other hand — literally – worked closely with me, seeming to desire fist flights. He often flew voluntarily to the glove. They were a deadly combination, as Sarah watched from above and Shogun bolted off the fist. Sarah would occasionally quarter the field as she soared on the wind. Only once was I able to take advantage of this quality by flushing a cottontail, which she took with grand style.

Often, I could call her into position. As I walked through some seven-foot tall sumac with Shogun on the fist, Sarah was 75 yards away in a tree. I spotted a rabbit in a form, so I yelled the escape signal along with her name. She came over 75 feet high. I waited for her to get upwind to flush the bunny which was caught almost instantly by Shogun. The cottontail ran downwind while Sarah rolled into a pumping stoop. She slammed into the quarry, but with the force of the stoop she lost her hold.

Several of Shogun's rabbits were straight off the glove. One such flight was near two brush piles. The terrier bolted the cottontail from one pile, only to have Shogun miss it as it entered the second. Shogun skyed up and hovered briefly as the dog charged in bolting the bunny again. He quickly took the quarry by the head. But the rabbit still did a one-and-a-half somersault with a half twist, and landed right on Shogun's head. Another fist flight was in tall swampy cover five-to-seven-feet tall. The rabbit bolted right at my feet. The tiercel flew straight out off my glove which I held over my head. The bunny burst out four feet, then turned back toward me. Shogun caught him literally between my boots. From her lofty vantage point Sarah often caught bunnies that I never saw. Many times she would catch cottontails that tried to sneak ahead, around or behind. A hard tail-chase usually resulted with Shogun jumping into the chase.

Alternating Stoops

Some of the most exciting and deadliest flights resulted from alternating stoop flights. In Indiana's tough, dense cover — much the same thickness as the Harris' wild habitat – one hawk can rarely continue a flight after an unsuccessful stoop. In a cast, however, each hawk can follow the other after a miss. One picturesque flight occurred when the hawks chased side by side. As the rabbit reached cover, they pitched up together with their wings and tails spread as each looked over its shoulder. One could almost hear the rabbit muttering something about its Last Will and Testament. At that moment the terrier arrived and bolted the cottontail as the hawks rolled into pumping stoops. The result was predictable and fatal.

One afternoon in fading light we hawked a railroad track. We flushed a rabbit that ran along the rail. Shogun bolted off the fist, striking on it within the first 10 feet. It evaded him with a quick side-step. Sarah, dropping from her perch on a tall pole, whirred past Shogun toward the still-fleeing quarry. She made the second stoop as Shogun rejoined the chase. Once again the bunny was equal to the task, eluding Sarah, who hit the gravel with a rumble. Shogun then roared by her, chirping encouragement as he pressed home the chase. Each hawk pitched up, then stooped time and again during the length of the 100-plus-yard flight. The rabbit's luck wore out when he tried to jump a rail and cross the track to a hole. Just as it began a leap, both hawks slammed into the it.

Cast flights also show the Harris hawks' cooperation. When Shogun caught a rabbit, Sarah wouldn't go in and grab it. She would land a few feet away, watching intently. A few times the quarry would kick Shogun and get away. From the ground, Sarah would explode into a ferocious tail-chase and catch it within a few feet.

A Make Hawk

Shogun enjoyed a great deal more success his first year than Sarah mainly because of her instruction as a "make hawk." At times their cooperation in locating elusive prey seemed uncanny. Once while hunting an abandoned farm with five men and a dog, a rabbit silently scampered undetected down a trail. Sarah caught a glimpse of it from her high perch. As she pursued it, the cottontail disappeared in the barnyard. When we arrived, both birds were stationed atop an old, sagging barn. As we worked the barnyard, Shogun bolted off the barn toward a wooden fence. He stooped at a slant but at the last moment shifted quickly, swerving around a small tree, landing and mantling on a small trail at the base of the fence. We saw the whole flight clearly but never saw the quarry. He flew hard — like he was pursuing small birds — yet none were present. A mouse was my next conclusion, as we walked leisurely to investigate. After all, there were no screams nor Shogun's usual rabbit wrestling.

Much to my surprise, he had caught and instantly killed a rabbit that was trying to escape along the fence. Later, I questioned him privately about this killing power, but he only muttered something about a Ninja death grip. I dropped the subject, thinking it really had something to do with his Cajun heritage.

Shogun's first flights at rabbits were close slips off the fist at an abandoned drive-in theater. He would fly up to them quickly but not foot them. At first, after 80-some small birds, I thought he may be frightened of this quarry. In retrospect, I think he was waiting for them to leave the ground. In his successful bird flights he would grab them on the rise. Shogun's attitude toward rabbits soon changed after Sarah repeatedly bolted in to snatch cottontails out from under his feet.

Cast flights were especially helpful on windy days. The pair learned to handle the wind, becoming stronger flyers while hunting on those days. Good field control — each hawk came to his or her own name — was a great help to get them in the best position on windy days.

Car-Hawking

Both hawks were trained through road-hawking their first summer. Shogun was much more successful than Sarah at starlings, pigeons and sparrows because — as a tiercel — he was quicker and more agile. Car-hawking never replaces the thrill of hunting in the field. It does, however, have its redeeming qualities. The birds became hard-penned in early July, but most fields are not huntable until late September. Therefore, hunting cannot be easily accomplished with a young hawk. With road-hawking one can hunt in a limited fashion. We hunted on private land which has a maze of industrial roadways. Some states have laws that restrict hunting in any form within a certain distance of a public roadway, so check your local laws before you ravish the neighborhood.

Car-hawking's redeeming qualities are that it:
• provides accessible legal quarry to train a young hawk,
• builds the hawk's muscles and stamina,
• develops a raptor's coordination and footing skills,
• enhances his desire to hunt and catch, when correctly rewarded, and
• increases the fitness both mentally and physically for larger quarry.

The transition from small birds to rabbits provided no real difficulties. The young hawk's confidence toward larger quarry was helped by this type of success on small birds. Once we switched from small birds to rabbits, Shogun still caught a few field-flight birds, but his interest decreased as his weight increased. A lower weight was necessary to motivate him to expend the energy necessary to chase small birds.

Road-hawking was accomplished by slipping the bird out the window of a moving vehicle at the birds along the road. Usually they were slipped at a speed between 15 and 20 mph. Starlings were the primary quarry, with 75 percent of Shogun's kills – the rest included sparrows, pigeons and crows. Road-hawking is best at dawn, when birds flock by the road for morning feeding. I started the young hawk by flying at flocks of five to seven starlings at 15 to 20 feet off the road. If the bird misses, we call him back into the window with a beckon. The flights were as hard as I made them – a longer slip produces a harder flight. Getting 20 or more slips a morning was common. If a young bird got a little discouraged because of misses, I gave him a shorter slip to end the morning with a catch.

The young hawks grew in confidence and stamina during car-hawking. When the hawk was slipped the birds flushed immediately. A short, ferocious tail-chase usually resulted. The slips were only at birds on the ground, usually on mown grass or harvested fields with short vegetation. The hawk learned to use the momentum of the car, turning it into flight speed. Shogun made a hard, direct flight at the birds on the ground. After it flushed he sprinted after it. He would rise up after it, following its every dart like a heat-seeking missile. If the quarry eluded him, Shogun would usually gave up the chase quickly as the starling skied up. If the starling made a level escape flight, the tiercel pursued for a longer distance.

He was rarely successful on flights that lasted more than 75 to 90 feet, though he often chased for 50 to 60 yards. The sparrow flights were short and ferocious with a quick conclusion, 85 to 90 percent unsuccessful.

During early training, close slips resulted in Shogun catching starlings on the ground. However, the best slips were long enough to allow the quarry to rise up, as the air strike was most desirable. This, however, allowed the quarry to pull its favorite escape maneuver when out-flown by the hawk. As Shogun reached out to grab the starling it would flip and slam itself into the ground, then fly back in the direction of the vehicle, which was stopped along the road. This slamming stunt was also a favorite maneuver of a crow when it's out-flown by a tiercel Harris. Shogun caught a few crows while road-hawking.

One exciting flight happened as Shogun was slipped at 20 mph at a lone starling taking gravel in a driveway. Shogun was slipped 25 feet up the road. The starling flushed immediately and pitched straight up. The tiercel was intense that morning and pumped hard striking him 15 feet up as it tried to dart to the left. The starling exploded like a bursting feather pillow. Shogun then parachuted down with his quarry.

The starlings' other escape tactic was squat low, then try to out-guess the hawk on which way it would dart, like a soccer goal keeper does on a penalty kick. Against an inexperienced hawk it usually worked. Yet with Shogun's agile footing he quickly learned to catch almost every bird that tried this. On one flight the starling froze. As the tiercel arrived the starling darted under his feet. Shogun grabbed at it, braked himself — while footing backward — and turned the back of his wings up. He then somersaulted. It wasn't a 10-point gymnastic maneuver, but Shogun enjoyed his feathered medal. Shogun performed this somersault a few other times, but it wasn't usually successful. However, what it lacked in efficiency it made up for in artistic value.

We had some cast flights at small birds in the field. On one very windy afternoon the tiercel pushed a sparrow hard along a chain-link fence. It darted through, trying to escape into a small bush. Sarah stooped off the fence, slamming into the bush, snatching the sparrow as it entered.

Solo Cast Hawking

Most of the time I handled the birds alone in the field. The only critical times were when they were fed either on the fist or on quarry. Then it was simply a matter of forethought, preparation and common sense. If the bird was to be fed on a kill, I would call the other bird to the fist. For a while I made the mistake of feeding Shogun on Sarah's kills. This only lessened his desire to grab the quarry first and encouraged him to accept a free meal ticket. When I abstained from this practice, he quickly learned to kill for his own reward.

Calling them both to the fist was as simple as placing a beckon on each glove, calling both their names. Obviously, I had a hawking glove on each hand.

Hawking With A Dog

A very successful addition to the cast was the rat terrier. Prince weighed 15 pounds and had long legs. We had hoped for a bolt dog, but he grew too large. This gamey little dog worked well in tough cover, bolted cottontails with great consistency from brush piles, and also flushed pheasants. Prince frequently made the difference between an empty and full bag. He was often "worth his weight in rabbits" — especially early in the season when the cover was very thick, and late in the season when cottontails were scarce. With his long, tireless legs he worked rabbit runs and brush piles all day without the slightest hint of fatigue. However, Prince was never opposed to sleeping all the way home in the warmth and comfort of the front seat. Rat terriers are sight dogs, primarily using sight rather than scent.

When Prince bolted a bunny he chased it until it put in or he lost it. If he lost it before it went down a hole, he jumped straight up into the air to look for the quarry. He also followed the hawks as they chased quarry. He often stood on his hind legs to look for a hawk after he heard the bells.

If the tiercel was pulled through tough cover while hanging on the hind end of a rabbit, Prince charged in and snapped the cottontail's neck. His killing style was from his rat-killing heritage. He never "worried" – played with or mouthed – the quarry; once it was dead, it no longer concerned him. In the field, his only concern was finding more quarry. Once in deep snow and tough cover we were flushing bunnies, but they were staying in the deep cover. With the hawks still in the trees, we heard a rabbit scream just for an instant, then Prince ran out of the briars. In the brush we found a fresh cottontail in the snow. Incidents like this were bound to happen with a dog so gamey, quick and well-bred.

After working a very large field we stood by the vehicles about to leave, when Prince ran back down a game trail we had just worked. When he yelped, Sarah sprung quickly off the vehicle, though she hadn't see a rabbit. She flew intently following the dog. Shogun watch her from the fist, then when Sarah was 75 yards away, he followed. Prince had long disappeared from view.

As we watched the birds fly away from us, I pompously turned to my friend said, "I'm not moving until I hear a scream!"

I casually leaned on my brush-beating stick while thinking their whole exercise was futile. My arrogance turned into humble excitement when we saw Sarah – now 250 yards away – stooping. As we ran over there we saw Shogun first. He sat in a large oak near some briars. He bolted to the opposite side of the briar patch, disappearing from view. Following the long run – which seemed in all the excitement to take an eternity – we found Sarah sitting empty-footed, except for some fur. Shogun was several feet into the patch standing on a rabbit with Prince trying to dispatch it.

Some Harris hawks seem to dislike dogs, but if they learn of the advantageous partnership, they will not only tolerate the dogs but rely upon them in the field. Sarah and Shogun responded to Prince's yelp as if I yelled the escape signal.

The Totals

The cast caught 191 head of game including 100 cottontails, 90 birds and a squirrel. Sarah took 69 rabbits, a pheasant, a few small birds and a squirrel. Shogun took almost all the small birds and 31 rabbits.

The quandary of flying a Harris in the extreme cold was definitely like holding a wolf by the ears: Whereas the cold presents a special problem for several weeks during the middle of the season, the major problem was not catching game but finding game to catch. We often drove 20 to 45 miles to fields to provide at least some game. Fox squirrels were the most available local quarry. I refused to fly Harris hawks at them.

Dealing With The Cold

A troublesome issue in northern Indiana was dealing with the freezing cold. The hawks were free-lofted in the mew, with its windows covered with clear plastic.

They were not housed together until mid-November after I reread

Sarah enjoys a pheasant she took in Merrillville, Indiana. The Indiana falconry regulations included a "let it lay" law for times when raptors catch a prey of the wrong gender or out-of-season. The falconry pheasant season was from September 1 to Feburary 28.

Floyd Presley's 1979 Hawk Chalk article on "Harris Hawks in Western Maryland." Presley wrote about free-lofting even unfamiliar Harris in the same mews. After talking with Floyd, I decided to house the Harris hawks together.

For the first 24 to 36 hours Sarah would wing-whip and push Shogun off any perch, no matter how low. She would even go on the ground just to make him move over. He fought back a couple of times, then he took his place in the pecking order. Sarah was raised by a red-tail foster parent. Shogun was hand-fed for a few days, then was placed with other Harris hawks to be raised. Oddly enough, Sarah would not hunt for a week after they were housed together. If she was in a tree and I walked under it or Shogun flew into it, she would fly off a hundred yards away. Her weight was correct. After that week, she started hunting again.

Having the birds free-lofted helped keep them warm during the cold weather, yet I still brought them in the house during the coldest part of the winter. Sarah, with her mature plumage and larger body, could be hunted and kept outside down to 0 degrees. Her weight in early fall was 32 ounces (907 grams) and in the coldest part of the winter, she flew at 39 1/2 ounces (1,120 grams) with good response. She caught one of her pheasants on a Tuesday at 19 degrees and 25 mph winds – a very cold wind chill indeed.

Shogun would only hunt down to 15 degrees. His immature feathers are not as warm as her mature plumage. My mistake was expecting him to cope as well with the cold as Sarah did her first year. This resulted in some foot problems. I should have brought him inside sooner. Harris hawks seemed to lose their ability to deal with the cold once they were brought inside. They didn't adapt to below 30 degree weather if kept inside.

Hunting with a cast of Harris hawks was a lot of work, but productive as well as exciting. Flying two hawks in this manner allows for hawking two birds in slightly more time than flying one alone.

I will never fly a Harris hawk alone; they were born to fly in a cast. For me cast flying is a dream come true.

HISTORICAL REFERENCE:

This article, published in the *1984 NAFA Journal*, was the first to mention car-hawking. Hoosier falconers Ted Nusbaum and Bill Boler invented the art of car-hawking in Osceola, Indiana. For more details see Page 150.

Jesse, a tiercel peregrine/prairie hybrid, holds her catch after a training flight near Fort Dodge, Iowa.

Chapter 4
Fence Jumping

Slick, black, Iowa mud weighted our boots as we trudged through yet another cut corn field. The tiercel hybrid's bell, which usually rung joyfully, only clanged to the sloppy trod. My disappointment grew with the lengthening shadows.

"This is not a normal Iowa winter," Jack heard me moan repeatedly that week. "It is hard to believe, a January without any snow and with such balmy weather.

"Another day without a slip," I grumbled, "If only we had snow."

Snow was the word. . . maybe the inoperative word for the week.

It was Thursday afternoon. Since Monday, Jack Mitch and I had been trying to hawk Hungarian partridge. He came on a promise of "a covey in every open field."

"Jack, it's as if these Huns were made for falconers. They are easy to find in the snow and they sit in the wide open. They're all over!" I had cheered as the phone lines danced to Indiana.

Jack's first year tiercel peregrine, "Bogie," had caught its first wild quarry on Tuesday. It was his first Hun flight. My tiercel, "Jesse," flew at Huns that afternoon, but a wild gyrkin interrupted the flight. Jesse attacked the larger falcon and they became interlocked 100 feet up, then tumbled to the ground. On both Wednesday and Thursday morning we had flights for Bogie, but none for Jesse.

It was a very frustrating week. Without the normal January snow, we had to walk the likely fields and pray that we would flush some Huns and mark where they landed. Marking was the hard part. The partridge would often fly over a slight rise and then put in. If their exact location was not known, they were very difficult to flush with a falcon overhead. Thursday morning when Bogie was up, we were within 15 feet of the covey. They wouldn't flush. That was finding the partridge the hard way.

With the snow cover we had in December, the coveys were spotted from the road. They resembled organized dirt clods. Each covey flushed wildly unless a falcon was aloft, so the falcon was released at a distance to climb above the quarry, then we went out to flush the partridge.

"It seems I rehearse this every time we work another field," I thought to myself, glancing at Jack.

He stood on a high spot in the road so that he could mark the covey if I flushed one.

"If only we had snow…" I lamented, trying to shake the heavy mud from my boots.

A partially eaten ear of corn sat at my feet as I began trudging again. The whir of sixteen wings thrashed the air as the covey rose 10 feet in front of me. The covey of eight clucked as they rocketed east over the road into a soybean field. We watched them set their wings and turn into the southerly wind. All the frustration was forgotten in our anticipation of the fight. We watched the covey put in the other side of a farmstead.

"Mark their location carefully," I warned myself, before walking briskly towards Jack.

"Were you able to see them land?" Jack asked as I approached the car, "I couldn't. They flew around the buildings."

"They're by the last barn," I replied, "Turn the car around!"

Jack drove urgently around the farmstead to the road, upwind of the partridge. From the shoulder, I stood with the falcon on one hand and the binoculars in the other scanning the field. The harvested soybean field contained no cover but the "gray partridge" had melted into the long shadow of the barn. We knew they were there, just 200 yards away beyond the fence.

"Should we ask for permission?" I asked, knowing that we should. I didn't want to be deprived of this well-earned slip.

"It is so close to the farm," Jack replied, "We'd better ask."

"Use all your charm, these slips aren't coming too easily," I said sternly, never taking my eyes off the field.

As Jack drove up to the house, a friendly German shepherd greeted him. An elderly man, dressed in faded blue overalls, appeared at the door.

"Good. Someone is home," I thought, turning back to scan the field.

Raising the binoculars, I began to rehearse the flight, as a golfer visualizes each shot before he swings.

"They're about fifty yards east of the last barn, either side of that little roll in the field. After we jump the fence I'll pull his braces and leave the hood on. Jesse will whimper a little with anticipation. Jack will walk down wind of us. Forty yards from the fence I'll unhood Jesse. He'll rouse mute and cast off." I paused to mentally watch him climb. "First he'll swing low to the east crosswind, then turn back west cutting in front of us. Pumping continually, he'll climb past us straight into the wind, then drift back over head. That will pin the Huns so we can move closer. In this wind Jesse will climb to about 250 feet. He'll swing in and out of position as we walk ahead. When Jesse is a little upwind, we'll make our last rush to flush the covey downwind. Jesse will twist into the wind, pumping into the stoop, then. . ."

"Hi, I'm Jack Mitch and we are falconers from Fort Dodge. . ." Jack began pointing toward me.

"You're what?" the elderly farmer asked.

"Falconers. We train hawks and falcons to hunt," Jack informed him. "Today we're looking for Hungarian partridge. . ."

A sinking feeling crept over me as I watched from the road. The usual, "Sure I can't see what you'll hurt!" was not coming in short order.

I had rehearsed the information often, "It's much harder to catch them with falcons than it is to shoot them. We don't use guns. The only thing I carry is a little pocket knife, and I'm afraid I'm not too dangerous with it!"

"Falcons, you say. . ." the owner asked, "And they come back to you?"

"Yes, they do," Jack responded.

"That is very interesting. . ." the owner said then paused to reflect.

"Would you like to see one?" Jack asked, feeling a bit more optimistic.

"I don't think so," the elderly man said slowly.

"Would you mind if we walked in your field?"

"I don't think so," the elderly man said uneasily and abruptly closed the door.

Jack's walk told the story even from a distance.

"He told us 'No' didn't he?" I said as soon as Jack drove close enough.

"Yes," Jack said without any tone.

"He said 'Yes, we can,' or 'Yes, we can't,'" I quizzed.

"He said he didn't think so."

"Did he say, 'No?'" I asked pointedly.

"He said he didn't think so."

"Let's fly them," Jack said flatly. "It will only take a minute and we'll be gone."

"Blast it all. . ." I grumbled glancing up at the fence.

"I could release Jesse from here," I said looking back at the ground. "Then I'll have to follow him into the field. That's legal."

Starting to look up, I turned away. The fence would be too small an obstacle to look toward the covey again.

"After all Jesse needs a flight," I reassured myself with my back to the field.

"It's too late to find another covey," Jack said solemnly. "It's now or never."

"He said 'No'," I paused. "And it's his property," I said reluctantly, opening the door of the car.

"So... We leave?"

"The farmer is surely watching us," I continued convincing myself. "If we jump the fence we would throw black Iowa mud in the face of every falconer and sportsman."

As we drove away, a red and orange sunset blossomed on the horizon of the north Iowa plains. Was it mocking or comforting us? The red beams brightened Jesse's salmon-colored breast as he scratched his hood, ringing his bell.

Will I sleep tonight? I wondered turning to stare out the window.

One day, that farmer will learn of falconers, I reflected, while watching the red hues melt into orange, *and remember them as kind sportsmen who ask before they hunt and quietly drive off when the uninformed say "No."*

Jesse, a tiercel peregrine/prairie hybrid falcon wears his hood.

Chapter 5
The Falconer's Psalm

The falconer is my companion,
I shall not be in want.

His patience encourages me to the
     extent of my abilities;
His forgiveness hardens my muscles to excel.

His desire is my desire,
His courage is my courage;
As seasoned warriors we respond as one
     to pursue our prey.

Even though I fly through storms and
     toward hardy quarry;
I fear no harm; He is with me.
The feel of his glove, the gentleness of his voice;
They comfort me.

He shelters me from all my enemies,
He has prepared a banquet of my favorite game;
My crop is full.

Surely health and success will follow me
     all the days of my life;
And I will dwell in the mew and heart of
     my friend forever.

Adapted from Psalm 23

Sarah with a black-tailed jackrabbit she bagged at the 1984 NAFA Meet in Lamar, Colorado.

Chapter 6
Hawking Lamar Jacks
Harris-Style

For falconers interested in a black-tailed jackrabbit hawking trip, the 1984 North American Falconers' Association Field Meet in Lamar, Colorado was just the ticket. As an eastern hawker with primarily cottontails to hunt, the thought of catching super-rabbits had always enticed me. With great anticipation, I planned a family vacation in Colorado at the same time as the NAFA Field Meet. The number of jackrabbits at the NAFA Meet was anything but disappointing.

Our primary hunting group was Harris hawkers from Louisiana and Washington state. Tom Coulson, Dr. Neil Smith, Joe and Brenda Turner and their son Todd were all from Cajun country. Toby Bradshaw, Jerry Fraulini and Dave Baker were from western Washington. We hawked with the Gehrleins and the Presley clan on occasion. One of the highlights of the Meet was to hunt again with the Kentucky boys including Tony Englert, Keith Hix and the crew — what a bunch!

Gang Hawking

We hawked in "family groups," sometimes called "gang hawking."

Family groups are both enjoyable and sporting especially at field meets. Wild Harris hawks — with their gregarious temperament — lend themselves to this style of hunting in groups of eight to ten. This temperament leads us to cast flights and family groups hawking in the falconry setting.

In Lamar we often had eight to twelve birds in the same field; but when we did, we would break into two groups of four to six hawkers and divide the field among the groups. Remember, the Lamar fields were not the small industrial lots like those at the 1979 NAFA Meet in Indiana. The Lamar fields were the size of. . . oh say, half of Indiana. That would be a small Colorado field. When we chased jacks, we used the whole field too!

During the trip several items amazed me. I had assumed that jackrabbits were just large cottontails. But jacks would materialize out of nothing in open fields. They were found in dusty pastures that were not overgrazed. They most often were bumped from their forms under yucca or sage. We also tried to hunt around winter wheat — the only green growth visible in Colorado.

Most days were warm, short-sleeve weather, with very cold nights. The wind was only really brutal a couple of days, but on most days it was a factor. Even on the windiest day, the improvising falconer could still catch game with a little help from his friends and the "Jackrabbit Express" — more on that later.

Turning a Jack

When hawking jacks the most important factor was for one bird to catch up to and turn the jackrabbit. The black-tails don't go to ground. Their escape method was rather simple yet effective: They just hotfoot it to the next county. Added to their quickness afoot was their tendency to run uphill and upwind.

While hunting one pasture, Neil Smith had his cast of female Harris hawks and we were in the center of a line of hawkers. We bumped a jackrabbit ten yards into the field and it bolted straight away. My Harris Sarah was the first to the jack and turned it left.

She shot up pumping into a wingover, turning it again this time to the right.

As it eluded Sarah's stoop, both of Neil's hard-flying hens hit it.

On another day soon after we separated into two groups, our group could still see the other group on a distant hill. On occasion, they would yell and we knew they put up a jack. Once a jack ran right toward us as we crossed a fence. We froze like stone statues over the fence and prayed the hawks wouldn't bate. The jack ran under the fence 20 yards from us when Fraulini yelled, "Ho!"

The jack eluded the first pass or two, then jumped straight up. Tom Coulson's Harris, "Fourth String," slammed into the jack's head in the middle of its vertical maneuver. My tiercel Harris, "Apache," applied the stretch when they hit the ground. This was a classic case of out of the frying pan and into the fire.

On Tuesday, I spent the afternoon with the Kentucky boys — the term "boys" is no insult. It was a badge of honor for those great hawkers. Tony, Keith and I flew our female Harris hawks and Dave Campell held Apache.

Quickly, we bumped a jack that ran 10 yards and, as the hawks closed in, it pulled a tight 360 degree circle. All the hens stalled out in the sharp turn, but as the jack completed the circle the tiercel whirred around and grabbed him by the head. The hens then assisted on the gang tackle. After the tiercel scored, I traded with Dave, and he walked Sarah. Dave then promptly bagged the second jack — with

Sarah. I traded back, but Keith scored next with his female, "Cody."

Black-tailed jackrabbits seek shade in the heat of the day near Dodge City, Kansas.

The Jackrabbit Express

Wednesday was the worst day for hawking because of 25-plus mph winds that danced across the prairie.

Hunting prospects weren't favorable as three-quarters of our time was spent going upwind to work back downwind for slips. But that day was saved by the invention of the "Jackrabbit Express." Joe and

Brenda Turner piled all the hawkers and birds in their truck and hauled us upwind a couple of miles. We then hunted fields on one side of the road, then the Express lugged us back upwind to hawk the other side.

One ever-present danger was the miles and miles of barbed wire fence. Most fences had four strands of wire, all of which were dangerous to a hawk chasing quarry. Jacks often used the fence as "cover" in this coverless terrain.

Dirt Hawking — Literally

At one point on Thursday, we crossed a wide plowed field toward greener pastures. I was quite bored with the crossing when brown blurs with small black flags started appearing out of furrows. Jerry's intermewed Harris, "Yiko," caught two jackrabbits in the first 60 yards. Coulson's female scored on a jack as Jerry was picking Yiko up off her quarry. Smith's female scored right in front of Sarah. All that was impressive enough, but it was Toby's female that took the show on the dirt track. She did the work that resulted in two jacks being taken next to a dangerous fence.

Forty yards from the end of our plowed gold mine, we bumped yet another jackrabbit that ran toward the fence. Toby's hawk chased closely pitched up and stooped over the fence. The jack, trying to evade her, jumped straight up, a maneuver that had been successful several times. However, Sarah was so close that she promptly planted her talons into it while it was three feet off the ground. Thirty yards into the next field a few jacks flushed. Toby's bird flew one jack down quickly as it approached the same fence we had just crossed. She grabbed it solo just this side of the fence and was promptly pulled under the fence. It was a close call but she was unscathed.

Sarah caught a jack solo and upwind, interrupting a pleasant conversation with Marvin Presley about hawking with small Jack Russell and rat terriers. That jack streaked upwind and, of course, toward a fence. Sarah didn't close the gap until 100 yards out. When she did, it was at the first fence. It passed under the fence and through a ditch, then up onto the road, where she applied four points of her eight-point acupuncture program. I threw down my hawking bag and scrambled over the fence, only to see her disappear into the other ditch. As I reached the ditch, she was being pulled up into the next field under yet another barbed-wire fence. Leaping — well, crawling — over the last fence, I watched, ready to pounce. She only had it by one-foot. The jack eluded me as it spun her in every direction. Finally I dropped to the ground and after a couple of grabs managed to get some fur. A little applied chiropractic treatment brought him into submission.

The Count

That week, Neil caught 15 jacks with his three females; I caught 12 jacks and three cottontails with my cast. But Yiko, Jerry's intermixed female Harris, made us look like we had watched ESPN at the motel all week. Yiko took 19 jacks and three cottontails — what a week! At least 10 of her jacks were solo. Yiko, an average-sized female, was quite fast, but her greatest quality was her footing ability. She rarely missed when within striking distance. The other hawks' only hope was to be closer to the jack than Yiko was when it flushed. If the other birds missed, Yiko wouldn't. She was a very determined bird. The only one more intense was Jerry. He kicked every bit of cover looking for quarry. Yiko was a second-year bird that had never killed a jack before the Meet. In fact, her first year she flew down and grabbed a Washington jack but was bucked off. From then until the NAFA Meet she refused every jack.

The Best Flight

The best flight of the NAFA Meet was not on a jackrabbit. We were hunting in the Comanche Grasslands and had just rejoined our groups. We were flying at least 10 birds with Neil flying all three of his hens at once. Neil was 150 to 200 yards away when we bolted a cottontail. After jackrabbit hawking the birds took to cottontail like white on rice. You could see the excitement in their rapid wingbeats and eager turns. At the rabbit's first hop the sky was dark with Harris hawks, like 10 heat-seeking missiles all intent on the same target. Yet, apparently this bunny experienced the same optimism as the ancient general who was pinned on a beach by the opposing army. His officer lamented, "We're pinned with no retreat and the sky is dark with arrows." To which the general calmly responded, "At least now we can fight in the shade."

This rabbit must have thought, "At least now I can run in the shade." He hopped, twisted, turned and even at one point stopped to allow a Harris to hit the ground in front of him. He darted back and forth in a very small area and was not touched once. Neil's hens came on the rise only to put the bunny down a hole while the other birds sat panting, "Which way did he go?"

The Lamar Meet was an experience with great hawking, fine friends and lasting memories.

I hope to visit Lamar and its kind people again soon.

Bradley Bisdorf holds Hunter, the Jack Russell Terrier with a snowshoe hare he caught in the Upper Peninsula of Michigan on January 1, 2007.

Chapter 7
Terrier Dreams

Prince slept on the passenger's seat as I drove home on the last day of the hawking season. The terrier growled and twitched while sleeping under Sarah, the female Harris hawk that sat on the head rest above him.

She had a full crop, and Prince slept hard while warming up after his trudge through wet snow. The pair had bagged four rabbits on the final day, raising the season total to 100, including cottontails and a few jackrabbits. She glanced down at him when he let out a soft rumble, and I wondered what he was dreaming about. Several incidents rolled through my mind as the van rumbled through the countryside during the two-hour drive home.

Briar Debate

Maybe, he was reliving that snowy day when a friend went hawking with us for the first time. After a few misses on rabbits near some heavy thickets, Sarah sat in a tree about some eight-foot tall briars. She was leaning forward and making several low chirping sounds.

"You see her?" I asked my friend.

"Yes," he replied with the tone of, "What do you think I'm blind?"

"No, do you see what she's doing?" I continued. "She's telling us that there is a rabbit in there. She wants us to flush it and she'll catch it."

"Yeah, right," he said in disbelief, proving that two positives can be a negative.

"Well, I'll prove it," I said, and the challenge was on. "Prince, come boy. In."

With that Prince ran back to us and I pointed him into a small hole in the briar. He ran in, and I heard a muffled noise and seconds later he ran back out.

"Well, that's just great," my friend mocked.

"Don't you know what happened?" I rebuffed.

"What."

"There's a dead rabbit in there," I said.

"Sure there is."

"Prince ran in, found the rabbit that was more afraid of the hawk then him, so it won't leave the briar," I said. "He grabbed it by the head and killed it. He left it there because terriers leave the victim to find another."

"Oh, really," he said laughing.

"OK, I'll prove it," I said as I took off my hawking bag and hung it on his neck.

I crawled on my stomach into the briar where Prince had been. My feet were still sticking out of the hole when I found the freshly killed rabbit. My friend was very surprised when I pulled it out of the briar, and even more shocked when I stuffed it into his coat for him to carry the rest of the afternoon.

Apache's Ride

While hawking a thin strip of brush between a plowed field and a country road, Apache, a tiercel Harris hawk, pursued a cottontail into some saplings and grabbed it by the closest end — the posterior. The rabbit continued through the tiny trees while banging Apache's wings on the saplings. Unable to transfer to the head of the quarry, Apache just hung on. Prince, apparently seeing Apache's dilemma, darted in on the rabbit, snapped its neck and was back hunting before the tiercel could get from the back of the bunny to the front.

Becoming Prey

Sarah would attack and drive off a dog of any size. But she grew up with Prince and considered him a castmate. However, on occasion Sarah would grab him. If game was plentiful, she was fine, but if he failed to produce quarry for 30 minutes — which thankfully was rare — she would bind to him. When she did, Prince would instantly drop to the ground and put his feet up by his face. He would freeze as still as a possum, seemingly realizing that struggling or growling would only increase the pain. I could always see him peering up from between his feet as I approached to gently pull her off. As soon as he was free, Prince would bounce to his feet and run down the rabbit trail as if nothing had happened.

State Police

That fall we were hawking on a drizzly, muddy afternoon on the edge of a larger, northern Indiana city, when an Indiana State Trooper pulled up to my van and flagged us over. I called down the cast of Harris hawks and walked through the muddy field to his patrol vehicle. The trooper — decked out in his well-pressed uniform with a bright shine on his boots and gold glimmer on his badge — stood regally next to the open door of his immaculate cruiser. What the trooper did not know was that Prince only knew two things about vehicle doors. Rule 1: If you're inside and the door is open, get out. Rule 2: If you're outside and the door is open, get in. As the four of us approached the trooper, Prince saw the open door and reacted according to Rule 2. Seconds later the spotless leather seats were covered with muddy, terrier prints. I never realized he could make so many paw prints on both front seats in 2.3 seconds.

Somehow, explaining Rules 1 and 2, did not offer much consolation to the officer, who — in spite of the mud incident — freed us to keep hunting.

Attack Dog Tackled

A couple weeks later, the four of us were hawking a semi-residential area of a small town where we had permission to hawk a feral field between two houses. A lady from the adjacent house — that did not own the field — opened her door and stared at me holding Apache while Prince worked the short brush of the open field. Sarah held her high perch in a tree on the fence row between the field and the other house. She was about 80 yards away.

The woman then opened her door and pointed toward us. A medium-sized dog charged out of the house, ran down the yard toward Sarah, then turned on to a path that ran directly at the three of us. As soon as it made the turn, Sarah jumped from her perch and flew the running dog down like a golden eagle taking a wolf. As the aggressive dog came within 30 yards, it was completely shocked when Sarah slammed into the back of its head. She bulldogged the dog into the ground like a cowboy tackling a steer. He made a complete flip, which knocked Sarah off. The terrified dog ran straight toward the house door, zigging and zagging like a running back heading toward the end zone, with Sarah shadowing its every move. The lady opened the door, he ran in, and Sarah landed on the awning over the door. She stood on the edge, bent over, staring at the closed door, apparently hoping the dog would return.

The woman uttered some things that a lady should never hear.

Missy's Mistake

A fifth member joined our hunting crew when a lady in the church wanted a new home for her 6-month-old, 11-pound terrier mix. She wanted to get rid of Missy because she was "attacking her cats." I then began flying a cast of Harris hawks over a brace of terriers. On one of our first outings, we flushed a bunny from a large brush pile near a subdivision. The rabbit ran across the mowed grass toward a house then darted around the corner of it into some shrubbery. The hawks and dogs were in quick pursuit, as the cottontail made the corner, the hawks flew over the roof and stooped into the shrubs. The rabbit squealed. A dog whined. Moments later, no rabbit could be found, but Sarah was sitting in the shrub holding Missy's face with her right foot. Apache was sitting on a bush. Prince was watching from a safe distance. He had already learned the lesson Missy had just taken.

PHOTO BY MARTI FILKINS

Jack Russell terriers, Hunter and Alli, rest in the warm of the sunlight.

A Birthday Shoe

On January 1, 2007, I celebrated the first birthday of our Jack Russel Terrier, "Hunter" by taking him and our other terrier Alli for a walk in the swamp on my in-laws Ted and Wilma Brown's property. My stepson Bradley Bisdorf went with us.

Oddly there was no snow on the ground that year and the swamp was merely wet instead of frozen. As we worked the edge of the swamp, Bradley was on my left and Alli was near him. Hunter was on my right. The terriers buzzed through the brush in their usual excited manner. The trio were all out of sight in the thick cover, but I could hear them nearby.

Suddenly, out of the corner of my eye, I saw a white flash dart out of the brush on my right. I assumed it was Hunter, as he had just disappeared in that direction. I quickly realized I was wrong when a second white blur appeared in my peripheral vision. As I turned toward them Hunter overhauled the snowshoe hare as it ran through some dry swamp grass.

As I ran over to help, the hare broke free and bolted away from Hunter. He made three leaps and tackled the snowshoe by landing on top of it, holding it with his front paws and biting it.

Hunter has often shown his athletic ability, but maybe no more than on his birthday hunt.

Groundhog Day

My in-laws were having troubles with woodchucks one summer and were seeking a way to remove the pests. I suggested we give the terriers a try. One evening a groundhog was barricaded under a small porch. My preacher friend, Greg Steere, from Holt, Michigan, was visiting us that day, so he and Bradley each held a terrier on leashes. The dogs were placed to block the two escape routes.

The terriers were enjoying the visit to the country and acting as gentle family pets. They were happy to be at the Brown's and were playing with Greg and Bradley as if they didn't have a care in the word.

But the moment the woodchuck bolted from its hiding place, their demeanor instantly changed. Greg and Bradley released the leashes. From opposing directions the terrier reached the yearling at the same moment. One grabbed each end and instantly — like they had done with their pull toys – they jerked backward.

The deed was done.

Greg, an avid hunter, fisherman and outdoorsman, was surprised to see the dramatic transformation from loving pet to intense hunter.

Nip It in the Butt

My cast of Harris hawks, "Sadie" and "Samwise," grew up around small dogs, and since I received them our terriers have always been within sight. I assumed the transition into a hawking team would be fairly easy.

Early training around the yard went well, so one afternoon I took Hunter and the cast to a wooded area near a swamp. As usual, I pulled the hawks out of their giant hoods and released them on top of the van. I then opened the door and released Hunter.

It was a mistake.

I failed to consider Hunter's habit. When released to hunt he would sprint over 100 yards as fast as he could straight away from me. Then he would run back just as fast and the real hunting would begin.

As the door opened he hit the ground running down a two-track. Sam just watched him run. But the 25-pound terrier's fast exit triggered a reflex response in the young female Harris. Sadie bolted after him, in the belief that if it's running away she should catch it. White-tailed deer would later get the same treatment.

I yelled at both of them, but neither paid me any attention.

I ran after them.

As Hunter topped a hill, Sadie grabbed him by the butt.

The feeling shocked Hunter and he jumped four feet into the air.

The look on his face was priceless.

Fortunately, he survived the attack unharmed. But he spent the rest of the afternoon hiding under the brake pedal of the van.

His Sister's Pups

One spring, Prince went with me and my two sons, Micaiah and Andrew, to get some puppies from Franz, the German immigrant who raised Prince. The boys were just four and five. Franz had a gentleman's farm where he kept a collection of various animals. He raised European deer, swans, several types of ducks, every variation of pigeon, two kinds of doves, goats, sheep, several breeds of rabbits, and so much more.

We took Prince to see the three puppies and their mother, Princess. Franz had named both my dog and his. Princess was Prince's sister from the same litter. They were born to King and Queenie. Franz had an unusual knack with names. The three pups went to some falconry friends in Washington state. We put Prince in the van and I asked Franz if the boys could get a tour of his animals. He agreed.

Micaiah asked me what happened to Princess. She had one eye gone and some scarring on her face. I quizzed Franz, who told us that early that spring a huge raccoon had come on the property one night, and Princess took exception to it. There was a battle: The raccoon left the farm in a bloody mess, but Princess lost her eye in the clash.

The boys were intently interested as Franz told the lively story in an even tone.

On the journey on the dirt path between the barns and sheds, we came to a long lean-to. The hackles on Princess' neck went up as she uttered a deep growl and marched around staring into the open-sided lean-to.

"Something is in there," I said to Franz, who nodded his agreement.

"What should we do?" I asked.

"Let's find out what it is," he said with a calm demeanor.

I started looking through the assorted barrels, boxes, lumber and items, while Princess assisted in the search. Soon, I happened upon a brown, paper, 55-gallon barrel, inside it was some round metal tubing and a medium-sized woodchuck.

"I found it," I announced looking down as the hog stared back. "It's a ground hog. What should we do with it?"

Franz smiled, "Just dump it out on the ground."

When the woodchuck hit the ground, Princess ripped into it like a chainsaw through a conifer. The battle was intense, if short. And the greatest shock was seeing the gentle farm dog, that minutes before was nuzzling her pups and playing with two young boys, transform instantly into a lethal weapon.

Soon the woodchuck lay dead in the path, with Princess, bloody and panting, standing over it like a triumphant gladiator over his opponent.

Franz glanced at the boys to see how shocked they were by this primal battle.

"Dad, we don't want a puppy," one of the boys said. "We want THAT dog!"

Harley was named Harley Davidson Filkins, after the famous American motorcycle, by my wife Marti. He is a Jack Russell-Miniature pinscher-Chihuahua mix. He's just as special as he sounds. . . .

A black-tailed jackrabbit flees from the pursuit of Harris hawks near Dodge City, Kansas in October.

Chapter 8
Jackrabbit Rescue

When *Outside* magazine writer Tim Cahill spoke at the 1988 NAFA Meet Banquet in Amarillo, Texas, he shared my story about rescuing a drowning jackrabbit at the 1985 NAFA Meet in Lamar, Colorado. He used the experience for an article titled "Forgot My Pants, Lost My Mind" in *Outside* and it was also printed in the NAFA book *Bond With the Wild.*

Indiana falconer Dale Barnett and a Hoosier teenager named Johnny Maron — who operated the blowdrier — shared that experience with me. Ted Nusbaum observed the "hare dressing" by Johnny.

I shared this story with Tim to illustrate how falconers honor the quarry and want to see it caught, but according to fair play. For falconers it's not about killing the quarry; it's about seeing the hawk or falcon succeed.

My wife, Marti, illustrated this principle when a sparrow became trapped in our enclosed front porch. She opened the door and used a broom to escort the sparrow outside. The small bird panicked and darted around the room as she tried to shoo it away. Our Jack Russell Terrier, Alli, heard the commotion and arrived to see wings flashing and a broom waving. When the sparrow flew to her side of the porch, Alli leaped to try to grab it. She fell short. On the next pass, Alli jumped on the window ledge then sprung out toward the flying sparrow and snatched it out of the air.

The bird Marti tried to save was dead.

"Wow, way to go, Alli!" Marti cheered.

Later she added, "I would have felt sad for the sparrow, but I was so proud that Alli caught it. I was excited for her."

Before the NAFA Banquet, I asked Tim to not use my name, so he described my position as a preacher as "a pillar of moral authority in his community." This story is one portion of his article.

Tim retold my story in his unique style:

Cahill Retells Rescue

Most hunters, all but the most doltish fringe, speak about respect for the hunted. But a falconer's concern for the quarry is legendary. Consider the story of an individual I met in Amarillo. He is a pillar of moral authority in his community and, for that reason, has asked me not to reveal his identity. Let's just say that one fall day, on his annual hawking vacation he was out flying Harris hawks with several friends. This was in Colorado, and the friends were flying their hawks from their fists.

Now Harris hawks, I've discovered, are rare raptors in that they hunt in groups, using strategy. I imagine the scene was rather like the one I had witnessed out in the corn stubble near the Amarillo airport. I recall a rabbit being pursued by the hawks. Once again it had occurred to me that if game were the purpose, a shotgun would have served better here. We scared up a rabbit, shouted "Ho ho hawk!" and the hawks sprang from four fists as the rabbit bolted slow off the mark, but one of the pound-and-a-half birds came in high, another low. There were several ferruginous hawks cruising the field and my guess is that the local bunnies were used to this sort of thing — stopped short so that the high hawk overflew him. The second Harris came in only inches off the ground but the rabbit leapt a full four feet into the air.

Then it disappeared in a series of sharp angles and lost itself in the corn stubble, there was on the part of the falconers, some small grudging applause for the rabbit.

The scene was somewhat similar in Colorado that day: four men walking through a field, hawks on their fists. A rabbit broke, the hawks flew. The rabbit bolted toward the gravel road. Between the road and the field however was an irrigation ditch. The day was cold and turning colder. A thin skim of ice had formed over the water in the ditch.

The rabbit had no time for caution and attempted to run across the ice, which broke. Now we have four men standing around with hawks on their wrists looking down into a ditch with some consternation.

The rabbit was drowning. It attempted to crawl up on a ledge of ice that immediately gave way, plunging the rabbit back into the water. When it surfaced the third time, ice was forming on its head. The men were abashed.

It is true that only moments earlier these men had earnestly desired the annihilation of the rabbit, but this drowning wasn't nearly what they had in mind.

Someone, it was decided, would have to save the rabbit. The gentleman in question — a moral pillar of his community, remember — took the task upon himself. First he removed his boots and socks. Then it occurred to him that the water might be two or three feet deep. A man could spend the rest of the day wearing wet pants. No, best to take them off.

But his shirt and parka hung down past his waist, and for all he knew, the water could be chest deep.

The rabbit was weakening.

No time to waste. Get the clothes off and save the rabbit. Hurry.

Imagine the scene. Three guys standing around with vicious-looking hawks on their fists and one naked man shivering on the subfreezing, wind-whipped plain.

Which is precisely what greeted the elderly couple as they drove down the lonely road that paralleled the ditch. There was a slowing of the car and our falconer had the enduring impression of two pairs of eyes, feeling much of what a driver feels when a deer is frozen in the headlights.

"Geez almighty, Madge, it's some of them devil worshipers Geraldo was talking about."

The squeal of tires. A spray of gravel.

The postscript here is that the rabbit was saved, it trembled in the men's hands, badly chilled. If they released it, this rabbit was going to die of hypothermia. The hunting trip was cut short. The hawks were hooded and the rabbit was driven back to the motel, where it was warmed and dried by a blow-drier. It was later released in a large field where — if the coyotes haven't gotten it, if the wild hawks or foxes have somehow missed it — it's still alive, fat and sassy.

Nonetheless, I have a persistent vision of the maids in that motel gossiping: *"Don't know who they are, but they come here every year. Capture rabbits and style their hair. I think they're mad hare dressers."*

The man who swam naked for the rabbit was finally foolish enough to tell his wife about it. And now, every time he comes home from a hawking expedition with some matter of grave or amusing import to relay — *"Honey guess what happened today?"* — she replies in the world-weary tone of one who has experienced much in life and is not often surprised, *"You didn't get naked again, did you?"*

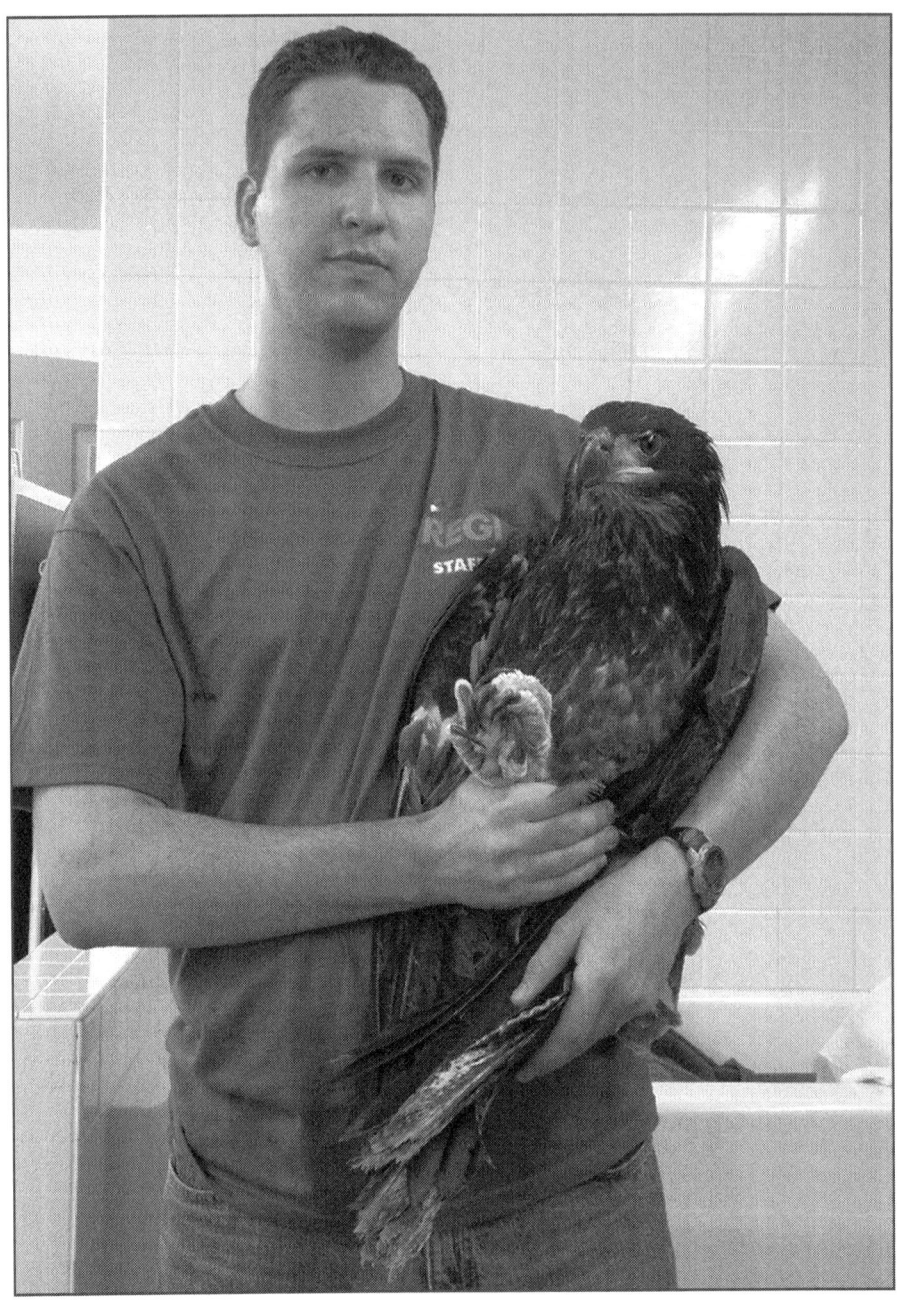

PHOTO COURTESY OF REGI

Nick Derene, a graduate student from the University of Wisconsin—Stevens Point, tracked Patty, the bald eagle, with high-tech equipment for three years. When she was released, Patty was outfitted with a satellite transmitter. Every four hours the satellite tracking device reported Patty's location to a computer that Derene monitored as a part of his graduate research program.

Chapter 9
WNV Bald Eagle Makes History

When my office phone rang on August 14, 2002, I never could had realized how historic a moment it would become.

Barry O'Connor, an autodealer in Pickford, Michigan, told me that a bald eagle was sitting on a new pickup in his auto lot. Barry knew I was the editor of the daily newspaper and wondered if I wanted to send out a photographer.

Moments later I was one the road, fearing it would leave before I traveled the 25 miles.

"It seemed like you couldn't hang up the phone fast enough," Barry told me later.

Unknown to me the immature bald eagle had caused quite a stir and every onlooker could get a closeup look at one of America's most majestic creatures.

At first sight it was clear that the eagle was in extreme danger. It sat stoic on the truck, allowing every visitor and photographer who dared within a few feet of it. Often it would close its eyes as if falling asleep. That action and its bizarre lack of fear made some visitors think that the bird was sick or starving.

It was both.

The national bird arrived at the residence of Rod Garvie, who lives just north of the car lot, the evening before while Garvie sat outside at a picnic table.

The huge, dark brown eagle flew over Garvie and landed in the yard. This activity struck him as very unusual. When he approached the young eagle, it seemingly walked along beside side him without much fear. The eagle then walked behind the garage and jumped up on a small out-building. Garvie wondered if it was hungry and wisely thawed out some smelt from his freezer to place next to the eagle. On

Wednesday morning, he found the eagle under the shelter of the out-building, presumably finding cover from the heavy rain during the night. The eagle jumped back on top of the short building but did not eat the smelt.

Later that morning, the eagle bathed in a puddle and then ventured over to a new pickup.

Fearing for the eagle's health and safety, O'Connor called a local vet, Dr. Clint Groover, and Ann Trissell, a local longtime wildlife rehabilitator.

Questions circulated among the crowd about the cause of the bird's strange behavior. Some wondered about West Nile Virus infection, while others wondered about lead poisoning or simple starvation as the likely cause.

I slowly approached the eagle and covered it with a blanket. She submitted without a struggle as I took hold of her feet. She was very, very thin. A quick exam revealed that she had no apparent wing, bone or joint damage. Whatever other problems she might have had, she was starving and needed skilled help.

Ornithologists claim that some 70 percent of birds of prey that leave the nest each spring die before they are a year old — mostly from starvation. Especially vulnerable are young eagles just after they leave the nest. This eagle appeared to be just such a youngster, with no white on her head or tail.

I held the eagle as Barry quickly transported us to the Pickford Veterinary Clinic where Barbara Groover took over her care until Ann arrived. I begged Dr. Groover to administer an IV dextrose solution to give the starving eagle a boost of energy that would allow it to start eating normal food again. Later that day the young eagle was transferred to Ann and soon it was eating smelt and regaining her strength and alertness.

Rehab in Wisconsin

By the weekend, Ann contacted the Raptor Education Group, Inc. (REGI) in Antigo, Wisconsin, and her husband Gerald drove the national bird there. Ann had named the bird "Patty" because "it works for the bird if it was a male or female."

A month later, REGI Executive Director Marge Gibson said that the gender of Patty was as yet undetermined and "we have not run a test to find out — We've been too busy caring for all the sick raptors (birds of prey) coming in to us."

"She is either a large male or a small female," Marge said. "But 'she' is doing much better."

When Patty arrived at REGI, her temperature topped out at the

PHOTO COURTESY OF REGI

Patty with her foster mom at the Raptor Education Group, Inc. rehab center in Antigo, Wisconsin.

thermometer's highest reading — 111 degrees.

"Her temperature was obviously much higher then that," Marge said. "But now she is down to 107 degrees."

Also, a blood test in August showed that Patty had West Nile Virus, which affects birds much like encephalitis does humans. It causes a brain anomaly and weakness in the limbs, which made it difficult for Patty to walk — without falling over — or to fly well.

Patty still could not feed herself, but Marge had placed her under the care of a foster parent, a 14-year-old bald eagle, who tore up food for Patty and fed it to her. The foster parent eagle was shot two years before in Wisconsin and her injuries kept her from being released, Marge said.

Patty had a long road to recovery because rehabilitation for a West Nile Virus infected raptor is like that of a human stroke victim. Flying, walking and feeding herself were all part of Patty's rehabilitation. After the long recovery — which may take as long as a year — Marge planned to transfer Patty back to the Eastern Upper Peninsula for release into the wild.

"But she still has a long way to go before that," Marge said.

When she arrived in Wisconsin, Patty weighted six pounds, two ounces, so Marge fed her chicken baby food through a tube to keep her alive. She was placed under the care of the watchful eye of her foster mom and weighed 11 pounds.

Months later Marge said Patty was flying again and the apparently feisty bird had her "spirit back."

Patty is not the only bird of prey the Wisconsin raptor rehabilitation center helped. Because of the spread of the West Nile Virus, the center received seven to 10 raptors a day that summer, Marge said. The raptor rehab staff was caring for some 30 bald eagles and another 150 "patients" — including other raptors and trumpeter swans.

The spread of West Nile Virus in 2002 had its greatest impact on the very old, very young and sick birds of prey. One Wisconsin facility lost 74 owls in three weeks to West Nile Virus.

Marge said there were "huge losses" of sharp-shinned hawks and great horned owls, and that she received a large number of Cooper's hawks, red-tailed hawks and some goshawks, along with the bald eagles.

The Second Year

On the anniversary of August 14, Marge was thrilled with Patty's recovery. In 2003 Patty was hunting and socializing well with a number of bald eagles in a 110-foot-long, 28-foot-tall building. The other eagles ranged in age from one-year-old, like Patty, to 30-years-old. This experience was preparation for Patty's return to the wild.

Patty became the most important research bird in the Midwest — and maybe the country — as far as WNV experts were concerned, Marge said. Because the long-term impact of WNV on an eagle's "language" skills — the way an eagle communicates during mating and within the complex bald eagle social structure — was as of yet unknown, Patty provided many answers after her release.

That winter, Patty was released into the wild near Sauk City, Wisconsin along the Wisconsin River. This area — instead of Eastern Upper Peninsula — had a wintering group of bald eagles that acted as a support group for the young eagle. Winter groups assist a young eagle in need. If Patty had been released in summer, all the adults would have had their own eaglets to feed. Concern for their own young would have kept the eagles from "adopting" other young birds in summer. After a winter group has formed, a laid-back attitude permeates the adults, and the older birds are willing to help younger birds through the winter.

Marge and Nick Derene, a graduate student from the University of Wisconsin-Stevens Point, tracked Patty with some high-tech equipment for three years. When she was released, Patty was outfitted with a satellite transmitter. Every four hours the satellite tracking device reported Patty's location to a computer that Derene monitored as a part of his graduate research program. This satellite tracking system — accurate to within two miles — followed Patty wherever she might travel in Wisconsin, Michigan's Upper Peninsula, Kentucky, or Canada.

Patty also had a second telemetry transmitter on her when she was released. During the following breeding seasons, Derene used the satellite information to get her location then used the short-range tracking telemetry to find her and observe her mating activities. It was hoped that tracking her behavior would teach researchers how eagles manage after recovering from WNV and returning to the wild.

Patty was the first WNV-recovered eagle to be returned to the wild and tracked to learn from her activities.

Released into the wild

On January 18, 2004, Patty was released back into the wild after a year-and-a-half recovery from the WNV. She took flight along the Wisconsin River while carrying some very high-tech equipment on her back.

It had been a long journey for her, but she did well.

At 2:30 p.m. she was released near a dam on the river, where a large roost of 300 bald eagles congregates each winter. The "warm" water from the dam provided open water and a fishing location for the eagles. Researchers were curious how the newly-released, young eagle would be accepted at the area called the Blackhawk Roost.

Upon her release, Patty promptly flew across the river and took a bath on the very cold day. After her bath she flew up to a roost to collect some sun. Soon, she was joined by a group of five immature eagles that apparently accepted her as one of their own. Then, the six eagles went off together fishing.

The researchers tracked Patty's movements through a 50-gram electronic backpack she carried. The REGI staff excitedly tracked her every movement several times a day through the computerized satellite data.

Satellite reports show Patty flew about 25-30 miles a day going up and down the river. After her first day, she hooked up with a group of adult eagles that adopted her. That was what REGI staff had hoped

REGI Executive Director Marge Gibson and an assistant put the tracking equipment on Patty before her release back into the wild.

when she was released in the winter.

While Marge and the REGI staff tracked Patty's activities from the raptor rehab center through the computer, students followed her on the ground with the radio transmitter.

"Your Sault Ste. Marie eagle is behaving absolutely normally," Marge said. "She fit into the wild group, literally, within minutes. We are interested in seeing if she travels back to the Sault this spring."

Two years later

"Her first two years, she resided in Escanaba, Michigan," Marge said. "She would roost in a large tree on a small island off the shore of Escanaba Bay. She got up early, very early in the morning then flew to shore and, I assume, began fishing."

One morning in early spring the four-year-old eagle flew to the Stephenson and Wilson area in Michigan's Upper Peninsula. But in April 2005, she stopped moving.

"We were concerned that something had happened to her and sent out people to find what we thought would be a carcass," Marge said. "The search party found her about nine miles southwest of Wilson. She was sitting on a nest. She was not in full adult plumage and was easy to spot and follow."

The eagle's inactivity was while she incubated her eggs. The female does most of the daytime nest sitting and while she left briefly to do some hygiene and exercise, she did not go far.

"Because the satellite was taking readings every four hours, even if she was off the nest for an hour a day we would not have picked it up unless it was at least four hours," Marge said.

Patty and her mate had two youngsters that first spring.

"This was amazing because. . . at that point, all the statistics told us birds that a recovered (bird from WNV) would never reproduce," Marge said. "Your little lady Patty showed the world that not only could she survive the West Nile Virus but could indeed mate and produce offspring. She did this all in the spring of her fourth year, which is very early for bald eagles to mate. Apparently, Patty was a very special bird even to another male eagle. We think — but have no hard proof — that she took up with a male that had lost his mate in some way. The nest she used was a traditional nest site and had been used in the past. The fact that they raised two youngsters as her first year as a mom would also point to someone in that pair having experience as a parent."

Patty's transmitter quit working soon after her family was observed so Marge has no additional information.

"I like to think Patty is out there still with her 'older man' having a wonderful life," Marge said with a huge smile.

So the young, sick eagle that sat on a new truck in O'Connor's parking lot became a national celebrity for raptor biologists and rehabilitators.

Patty's success was the result of the concern of several folks like Barry O'Connor, Ann Trissell and Dr. Groover.

Their compassion for one of our national birds resulted in making history in the Upper Peninsula.

Chapter 10
Khan of the Sky

Historical fiction of Mongolian falconry
Illustrated by Jeff Alkire

The snarl of the wolf thundered across the steppe, drawing the eyes of the five horsemen to the East, as an orange sheen of dawn rose over the snow-capped Mongol Mountains. All but one war horse whinnied and moved restlessly, as they felt the tenseness of their riders. On the calm horse sat a tall Mongol, whose firm face was covered with a well-trimmed beard that he stroked with oversized hands.

His demeanor commanded a natural trust and loyalty, from man and beast alike.

"He is only 1,000 yards away, shall we roust him out?" Jebe said to the Genghis Khan, anxious to have something productive come from this chilly morning ride. He stood in his stirrups and raised his hand to shade his dark eyes as he looked for the wolf. This slender warrior was the youngest General the Khan had ever appointed. Jebe was honest yet often tactless, but his loyalty was beyond challenge.

High above, the wolf's howl was greeted by the long, piercing scream of a golden eagle. The horses stood calmly and with one action all the horsemen looked up into the brisk blue sky and saw her golden feathers glow in the morning sun. The clouds raced across the sky behind her as the mountain winds beat against her. With a dancer's grace and a warrior's strength, she held her position above the horsemen.

"I will ride alone to observe the wolf," the Khan said. "Patience in a warrior, as well as a hunter, is a sign of wisdom, my young Jebe."

As Genghis walked his horse into the sunrise, the eagle shifted her position to follow him. For twenty minutes he ambled across the rocky steppe.

"Why must we delay? There is so much to do," Jebe lamented. "We have worked three months for this day. Is he so tranquilized by this ride that he has forgotten it is the last day of the Great Hunt?"

"Have you not just heard the words of your Khan?" Yaru reminded him. "Patience is a sign of wisdom."

This elderly general was a little envious of Jebe's early appointment and he occasionally let it out. Yet Yatu liked Jebe and saw great potential in him, and therefore he willingly invested time into him as the Khan requested.

"Yes, my stately general," said the thick-chested General Bator. "But were we more patient in our twenties?"

Bator questioned as he looked at Jebe with fatherly assurance and thought how much Jebe looked like his father, who died at Bator's side in battle.

"Isn't it true in Mongolia Empire, as it is in Arabia, that some are wise before their time?" questioned Nathan, a new missionary to the East. He was dressed in Arab pants and boots but his Mongolian coat and hat were from Jebe. Nathan thought of the warmth of the fur coat and Jebe's friendship, as he watched his horse's warm breath dissipate in the frigid air.

"Some are wise before their time, only if they observe," Yaru said.

"Yes, but one must be wise enough to take the time to observe to become wise," Nathan rebutted.

"Do all young preachers try to argue heathens into the church?" countered Yaru by changing topics.

"But, how am I to become wise while young unless I may learn from your wisdom, my stately friend," Nathan said, bringing them back to the subject.

"Now, you know why our diplomatic friend was chosen to join us in the Khan's daily company," Jebe said smiling at Nathan, feeling that he had somewhat vindicated his own youthful pain.

"Yes," Jebe answered. "But, I have always sensed that there is something more between the Khan and this eagle than the normal falconer and hawk relationship.

"On her first wolf kill," Bator began, "she grabbed a large female on the shoulder with her left foot. As she reached to plant her right foot on its head, the wolf turned, biting her foot. Neither would let go so the Khan quickly killed the pinned wolf with an arrow shot from horseback. Mongolian archery and horsemanship, along with the Khan's unshakable confidence, triumphed again! But her foot was severely injured. A rear killing talon was splintered half way up. It was a bloody mess. Genghis was noticeably moved, which was unusual for him.

"Kneeling beside the wolf holding her in his arms he drew his dagger and cut his hand, mixing his blood with the eagle's, therein uniting their spirits in Mongol brotherhood. He then carried her to our Chinese physician for treatment," Bator said.

"But what about last fall?" Jebe questioned as he noticed how far behind the Khan they were riding. "After one unsuccessful fox flight Shar-khan attacked the Khan himself. She circled behind and knocked him from his horse binding to his left shoulder. She then tried to bite his ear but when she reached down he grabbed her head. He then beat her head until she finally tried to change footing, then he spun himself free from her grip."

"We were nearby but were told not to interfere. It was a close one!" Yatu said lowering his eyes, shaking his head slowly.

"Genghis later told me," Bator added, "that he felt that this aggression was Shar-khan's retaliation for the time he released a fox, alive. After she caught the fox after a valiant chase, the Khan picked her up and released the noble fox. Shar-khan watched it flee and was never quite the same hunting fox afterward."

"You see, our two young apprentices, there is much to learn about hawks and life and how they are interrelated," Bator stated with no air of condescension. "He forgave her of this aggression, realizing that their relationship was a partnership, not that of a master and slave."

The Great Hunt

As they came to the yurt village the Khan dismounted and tied Shar-khan to her perch just outside his royal yurt. The Khan then remounted to ride to the steppe, as his Old Elite Life Guard, "The Bahadur," rode up to join him. They were dressed in black armor with a black kalat — a fur trimmed hat — with red facing. They were all mounted on black horses with red harnesses and saddles.

Nathan nudged his horse toward Jebe asking him in amazement. "Do all your warriors carry this many arms?"

With clannish pride Jebe turned to Nathan and said, "Only the Bahadur wear black, but all our men carry a wicker shield covered with thick leather, while on their left side they have two bows — one for long range and one for short range. On their right side they have two quivers each containing at least 60 arrows. Some of our special units carry whistling arrows for signaling and identifying targets, incendiary arrows and arrows tipped with tiny grenades that were developed by the Chinese. Each has a lasso hung from his saddle and a dagger strapped to the inside of his left forearm. Apart from these,

the light cavalrymen carry a small sword and two or three javelins.
The heavy cavalrymen carry a scimitar, a battle-ax or a mace and a
12-foot lance with a horsehair pennant and a hook below the blade."

"We have the best armed warriors in the world," Bator declared to
Nathan. "And may your God be with any nation that tries to stand in
the Khan's path."

"In the summer and fall of 1204, we conquered the Kerelt tribe,
gathering new recruits," Yatu said continuing Bator's thought. "As is
Genghis Khan's custom, he uses the Great Hunt to organize and train
the new troops and to keep us all sharp on our communication tech-
niques. Our superior communications and our disciplined troops
allow us to use special tactics in battle. These have made us, as I see
it, nearly invincible."

"The precision with which our troops perform their intricate
maneuvers on the battlefield is only attained after months of initial
drilling and continual practice thereafter," Jebe began, looking at
Nathan. "The tradition of instructing young boys in horsemanship
and archery is now an obligation under law. The most imaginative
method of training, however, introduced by Genghis is the Great
Hunt.

"It was conducted like a campaign and designed to create teamwork throughout the army, temper its discipline and swell its morale.
For us no other sport or military exercise could be more effective. It
is held at the beginning of each winter in peacetime and lasts three
months involving every soldier. Huntsmen mark out a starting line,
up to 80 miles long, with flags denoting the assembly points for each
lumen (unit) and hundreds of miles ahead of the line they plant
another flag to mark the finishing point. At the signal from the Khan,
the entire army fully dressed for battle, rides forward in one line driving all the quarry before it. As the weeks go by and the game begins
to build up, the wings of the army advance ahead of the center. When
they pass the finishing point, they ride in to meet each other, totally
encircling the quarry. Once the wings have met, the circle begins to
contract with the line deepening until, on the last day of the drive the
army becomes a huge human amphitheater with thousands of terrified animals crowded into its arena."

"At least unlike a war, you have fresh meat during the three-month
campaign," Nathan said.

"Quite the contrary," Bangor continued as Jebe tried to control his
restless mount. "Throughout the drive it is forbidden to kill, but it is
more than just a point of honor that none of the animals should
escape. If any man allows even the smallest of them to pass through
the line, both he and his officer are punished.

"At first the hare and deer test the soldiers' agility, but as the number of animals grows the predators in their midst become as terrifying as the army. The wild boar and the wolf packs are the next to try their courage. By day the officers ride behind their men directing the drive. At night, while half the army keeps watch, the rest sleep around their campfires fully-dressed and ready for action. On the final day the Khan rides first into the arena to take his pick of the game. When he has finished and he goes to a hill overlooking the army, it is the soldiers' turn. The animals that can be eaten are shot cleanly. With the whole army watching, it is an opportunity for men to show off and impress their superiors with their courage. Some hunt with a sword and some died fighting tigers on foot. A tradition has been established that at the end of that day, old men and young princes come to the Khan to plead for the lives of the remaining animals. When their request is granted the Great Hunt is over."

Morning at the Hunt

As they came over a small crest and they rode up to the army on the Temeen Ke'er (Steppe of the Camel) near the foot of mount Tulkinche'ut. At a signal from the Khan, flashing swords relayed a message, and with one motion the units began closing the circle on the harried quarry.

"One unusual note, Nathan," Yatu added, "is that there were no tigers this year, and there is no word of any escaping."

"Yet the pack of nine wolves has more than made up for the absence," Jebe said excitedly. "They have been killing roe deer almost since the outset of the hunt. This pack does not seem as disoriented as the ones I've seen in the past. Following their dominant male, they continued their hunting forays, seeming to enjoy our helpful, if overly ambitious, assistance. The Khan was pleased with the actions of their leader. At times he appeared entranced by watching them. I thought, at times that he even ignored the troops."

"But let any unit sway just one whisker on a foal's nose and his elaborate flag signals instantly reprove them," Yaru said. "This is the manner of our Khan: By observing the leadership of a wolfpack he absorbs all of their tactics and wisdom, and applies it to defeating his enemy, or maybe even the wolf himself."

Council on the Steppe

It was almost noon as Genghis and his four observers sat on horse-back on a ridge overlooking the Hunt, entranced again by the wolf leader. He had just killed the largest wild boar in a vicious fight when an envoy from the Ongut tribe rode up on his well spent horse. The envoy's name was Yoqanan or John — that is his Christian name. Nathan greeted John as a brother in Christ.

"Many of the Onguts have become Christians. Jesus' teaching is fil-tering throughout the whole Mongol world," Nathan commented to Yatu.

"It is not with missionary zeal that I have come today," John said after drinking some water from Nathan's flask. "Nagur-khan of the Nayman tribe has asked the Onguts to war with them against you, most honorable Khan. I have come to warn you and to pledge our support to you."

There on the steppe in the midst of the Hunt, Genghis spoke to the messengers who relayed his call to his generals. As they rode up and dismounted he began to hold council, it began with several minutes of chaotic chatter.

Kaban, an older General, then commanded attention and said, "It is spring... a time of year when the horses are too thin for campaign-ing. Any war expedition should therefore be held over until the sum-mer and autumn."

They usually left their encampment at the end of May, going down to the plains where the thick grass allowed their herds to make a gradual recovery from the winter.

However, the youngest brother of Genghis, Temuge-atchigin, demanded immediate action, "The horses are too thin? What is this excuse? How can we do nothing when we are brought such news?" The Khan then turned to the Sage with a questioning look, "It's a riddle, most honorable Khan: A soul above it, And a soul below With leather between, And swift it doth go."

Began the wise Sage, who answered his riddle after a short silence.

"The answer is a saddle, On horse with man astraddle."

Belgutel, the Khan's half-brother, spoke in affirmation of rich spoil. "The great herds of Nayman horses and the royal yurt will be left behind as — at our approach — their tribes will scurry to the tops of their mountains. To the horse! It is the only answer!"

"The Great Hunt truly gives rise to the morale and spirit of the army!" Nathan said to Jebe.

With a confident smile Khan agreed, "With such men about me,

how should I doubt victory?"

Nine Wolves

With that he mounted his horse, pausing to reflect upon the Hunt. Then without utterance he rode off toward his yurt. The units held position as Jebe rode after the Khan. When they reached the yurt Genghis flung himself from his saddle, grabbed his leather gauntlet, and lifted Shar-khan all in one sweeping motion and was remounted in no more than two swishes of a mare's tail. Only the rumble of hooves could be heard as they galloped back to the Steppe of the Camel.

When they arrived, the excited troops were waiting. The Khan rode up to a special unit of the Bahadur.

"The nine wolves," he said, to the Bahadur captain.

Only then did it strike Jebe that the wolfpack had the Mongol's sacred number — nine. "Has Genghis seen some kind of omen from our Mongol god, the eternal Tengri?" Jebe mumbled to himself.

"What did you say, Jebe?" Nathan asked as he watched the Bahadur, not hearing his response.

What happened next was only made possible by the horsemanship and courage of the Bahadur. The unit of twelve men rode into the circle as the whole army cheered their approval. For them the result of three long months of work was about to be harvested. The unit was swallowed by a sea of nervous animals. A bewildered stag charged the line of troops only to break its leg as it bounced off the horse and human barrier, as the Bahadur unit came upon the wolf pack, that took a stand behind their leader. The commander signaled archers outside the ring to fire incendiary arrows creating the smoke screen for which Genghis' armies had become famous. The twelve then drew grenade-tipped arrows startling the pack toward the west slope of the Steppe. The outer archers produced a smoke screen with amazing precision as the wolves were pushed closer to their exit. The screens kept the wolves separate from the other animals and also kept the others from the opening for the elite few.

It was only after the pack passed through the barrier that they acted as anything but one unit. Then the huntsmen released the dogs, which were handpicked by the Khan. They were often used to hunt not only fox and wolves but also tigers. They were large, muscular beasts by any standard. They had no fear of wolves, and each had scars to prove it. The wolves then abandoned the pack to seek their own safety from the dogs.

"The Khan is out of position," Jebe said muttering again. "He is in an unlikely place to slip the eagle at the fleeing wolves."

"Once again, the Khan will be rewarded for his intentful obser-vance," Bator claimed, "but now, it was Shar-khan who must match her courage against her dreaded foe."

Shar-khan and the Pack-Leader

The leader wolf ran toward the rocky terrain that the Khan had chosen. When the wolf was half way across the opening, a Bahadur fired a whistling arrow over the Khan. Genghis then rode out from behind the rocks, and Shar-khan launched instantly at the running wolf. The wolf veered to his right as the eagle began to close the ground between them. The Khan spurred his steed toward the encounter as Shar-khan covered nearly 200 yards to overtake the wolf. As she reached to foot him on the shoulder, the wolf tucked his head and buckled his foreleg resulting in a powerful flip. Shar-khan pulled out a large chunk of fur and flesh as she lost her grip and was rammed into the ground. The Khan cursed the day another wolf shat-tered her killing talon. The leader then scrambled back toward his original destination as Shar-khan rebounded to continue her assault.

Genghis cut off the wolf's escape as Shar-khan footed him on the rump. It was foolhardy of her but she was too intent on her quarry to be intelligent. As the wolf reared up she grabbed the middle of his back only to have him fling over on his side and knock her against a rock. He then twisted back over himself to try and bite her. Shar-khan lost her hold with her injured foot so the leader jumped up and spun around, trying to shake her completely loose. The Khan was close at hand, but the wolf's erratic movements made even the shot of a Mongol's arrow too hazardous for Shar-khan. Worse yet, the terri-fying cry of the leader had somehow reoriented his scattered pack.

Even though they were still pursued by the dogs, they ran toward their leader. The wolf then stopped spinning and turned the other direction snapping at Shar-khan again.

His teeth closed around the primaries of one wing, severely limiting her mobility. Even from a great distance terror could be seen in the Khan's eyes as he looked at Shar-khan and her adversary. He drew his bow instantly as only a Mongol could.

As the wolf reached to strike her with his claws, she jabbed him with her left foot, driving her talons into his throat and neck. It was none too quickly. He relaxed his grip, and with hackles raised, she stood up on her now dead enemy, footing him time and again in rage.

"Genghis knows better than to approach her while she was in such a mood," Bator noted.

The Khan sat on horseback savoring the moment of this victory when another whistling arrow passed over him.

The She-Wolf's Revenge

Seven of the wolves were killed along with four dogs in their wicked brawl. The pack-leader's mate had as yet eluded the dogs and bounded fearlessly toward Shar-khan. She was being chased by a bold hound, which had opened her right shoulder. Her gray coat glimmered with dog blood as well as her own. With that and her glassy eyes, she looked like a messenger from hell. Genghis lifted his bow and drew the arrow to his cheek. When he saw Shar-khan out of the corner of his eye. She flew directly toward the raging wolf. Genghis relaxed the tension on his bow as they approached each other. At the moment of collision, the she-wolf leaped high and with a satanic hiss. Shar-khan pitched up and looked as if she would slam the wolf in the face. However, she flared up out of reach and stalled out over the wolf. She then turned stooped at the wolf. The she-wolf looked over her shoulder and stumbled as she landed on the uneven ground. Shar-khan hit the staggering wolf binding to her head and neck.

"Once again the Khan chose the correct battle field. The rocky terrain was much to the wolf's disadvantage," Bator said, concluding his running commentary.

The Day's End

The day ended in the traditional fashion of the Great Hunt but the Khan was not present. He went to his royal yurt and sat with Shar-khan. Holding her close he looked deep into her piercing eyes as one would an intimate friend. A small fire flickered and cracked quietly as its light made Shar's golden feathers glisten. Jebe then saw a red tinge of wolf's blood acknowledging her success.

Jebe thought that Khan was contemplating the war that would begin tomorrow when he began to quote an eagle poem. He then remembered a Mongol proverb that Bator taught him.

"When your heart flies with the eagle, the mind returns to life's struggles, with clarity and courage."

" Surely," Jebe thought to himself, "the essence of falconry is not what happens to the quarry but what happens to the falconer."

Jebe's thoughts drifted back to the poem, as the Khan continued.

"...You are the Rule from the Indus,
to the black forest of Baykal.
And Khan over the great plain of China,
to the rocky steppe of Arkal..."

Tranquilized by this moment, Jebe thought of the eagle's broad domain.

"Will this Khan control the entire domain of his noble partner, the Khan of the Sky?" he asked himself. A smile crept across his face as he looked into the Khan's deep eyes.

"Somehow...I'm sure he will!"

The female Harris hawk, Sadie — named "Mercedes" by my wife Marti — turns her head upside down, as if trying to interpret our dialogue.

Chapter 11
Dialogue 101

A man's curious eyes followed me as I left the Farm and Fleet Store, with 12 quarts of 10W40 oil in plastic bottles. I hoisted them up on my shoulder and walked past him toward my van.

"Hey, is that your hawk?" he asked a typical question as he gestured toward the van.

"Yes," I said as I took the box from my shoulder, wondering how interested he was in falconry.

Maybe he has a rabbit field where I could go hawking, I thought, which consoled my impatience for this redundant conversation.

"What kind of hawk is it?" he continued.

A second typical question.

"Harris hawk," I said thinking of how the conversation will continue.

Next, he'll ask "Are Harris hawks from around here?" And I'll say, "No they are from the desert southwest." How many times have I been through this before? I thought in despair.

"Do you need to have a permit to keep them?" he asked.

Good question, so there is hope for a dull morning, I thought more cheerfully.

"Yes, a DNR permit." I almost added information about my file drawer half-full of papers, letters and permits.

Should I mention the two-year apprenticeship, test and DNR inspection? I mused.

"Someone flew them in a field near here. . ." he began.

That was me! I thought. I could see the screen of my favorite abandoned drive-in theater only 200 yards away.

Had he seen me yesterday when we caught a rabbit there? I wondered to myself.

"It was near my house. . ." he added after a pause.

"Oh, where do you live?" I asked as I thought of the trailer court that surrounds the drive-in.

"A few blocks from here on the other side of the viaduct. . ." he said.

Oh, he doesn't live near the drive-in and I went to that field by him once. That was the day she grabbed the . . .

". . . A couple years ago," he continued, "some guys were farting around in the field next to my house and their bird attacked my dog."

"Is that right?" I asked in mock surprise.

That was me alright. . . "Guys," why the plural? I was alone, except for my hawks. Was my presence so dominating that I seemed to be two people?

"What happened?" I questioned. A smile crept across my face, as I recalled that day. I remember wondering why his wife turned the dog loose on me. My hawk slammed into the head of the dog and rolled him over. She looked like an eagle attacking a wolf. The hawk tail-chased the dog back to the house where the lady threw open the door and the dog charged inside.

The hawk landed on the awning over door, as she uttered some words a lady should not say. I then whistled the hawk back and continued the hunt. After all, I had just talked to the landowner next door and received her permission to hunt there.

"Our dog was jumping up and down and he blew his whistle and his bird attacked my dog." he continued.

"Well, they don't usually attack dogs." I said, wondering if it was a little white lie.

"What kind of dog was it?" I quizzed, asking a question to which I knew the answer.

"A Springer Spaniel."

A Springer! All this time I thought it was a Brittany, I thought.

"Do you own the field?" I began in my own subtle defense.

"No."

"Did he have permission to hunt there?" I asked knowing I had it.

"No. . ." he said, again.

No? He didn't even ask his neighbor if I had asked to hunt there.

"The owner is a widow who lives in Chattanooga, Tennessee," he continued.

Wow. Had her husband died and she moved in the last two years? How old did she look, anyway?

I couldn't recall.

"Oh, do you live a few houses down from Carol Bledecki?" I questioned, thinking it's always good to change topics while regaining your balance.

"Yes." He answered with a puzzled look.

Was he wondering how I knew where he lived? He didn't know that there are only two falconers in this county.

"I do know were you live," I said as I remembered the landowner telling me her husband ran his beagles in their field.

I almost asked about the color of his dog, but I thought he might wonder why my curiosity was so specific. I thought springers were black and white, and this dog was liver and white.

Instead I asked "How big is your dog?"

He bent down and showed a height a few inches above his knee, "About this high."

"He caught a dog that big?" I said with my eyes wide with amazement. She had caught strange dogs twice that size. Dog catching was her greatest vice.

"Yes. He sure did."

"How did he train the bird to catch the dog?" I asked, knowing full well that he didn't even see me, much less know how the bird was trained.

"I don't know."

"Were you there?" I smiled, asking another question I knew the answer to. I was really enjoying myself, again.

"No, my daughter saw them and let the dog out."

His daughter! I always thought it was his wife. I didn't think that a mere girl could curse such a blue streak. At least my ears weren't cold that day.

"Next time she sees them farting around, I told her not to endanger herself or the dog and let her fingers do the walking," he said, as he gestured dialing a phone. "Let the guys with the badges take care of them."

"That's for sure," I nodded and thought I'd wait for another day to ask if he had a rabbit field I could hunt.

Sarah Kedar

Chapter 12
Sarah Kedar
A Memorial to the "Princess in Black"

The words carbon monoxide will always inflect piercing pains of guilt, grief and loss by the remembrance of our separation.

I won't remember that lonely night when I woke to check you, then covered you that final time with a towel as a shroud.

I WILL REMEMBER. . .

. . . your morning greeting when I called your name.

. . . your first pheasant on our first Thanksgiving Day together.

. . . the thrill my brother and I felt at your first crow kill.

. . . your first season when you caught only 22 head in almost daily hunting from July to February.

. . . our struggle to succeed and the oneness it brought.

. . . the two times you caught four rabbits in less the 20 minutes.

. . . your desire, heart and faithfulness.

. . . having you pitch-up and return to the glove at only the call of your name.

I'll even remember when you caught that elderly lady's little poodle and she asked if *you* were OK! I'm sure that mine were not the only tears for you and that there were more than a few spontaneous moments of silence in your memory.

The great joy of having known you makes the pain of losing you more intense. However, the joy of being with you *is* worth all the pain of my loss. I would rather endure the anguish of losing you than to have never known you at all. The knowledge of your uniqueness gives me the strength to become vulnerable again so that I may see another's specialness as I've seen yours.

Your memory is one gift of God that death cannot destroy.

In Hebrew, Sarah Kedar means "Princess In Black."

Sarah Kedar

Sarah Kedar
A Sonnet to a Lost Love

Should you go first and I remain
To walk the fields alone,
I'll live in memory's pleasant mews
With the fervid flights we've known,
In Summer I'll dream of open skies
seeing you silhouetted in blue,
In early Fall when brown leaves fall
I'll catch a glimpse of you.
Should you go first and I remain
With quarry to be sought,
Each perch you've touched along the way
Will be a hallowed spot.
I'll hear your voice,
I'll feel your touch
Though blindly I may grope,
The memory of your out-stretched wings
Will lift me up with hope.
Should you go first and I remain
To hunt alone this year,
The memory of your faithfulness
Will give my life some cheer,
Our oneness brought such happiness
Our days were filled with joy,
And memory is one gift of God
      that death cannot destroy.

Adapted from the anonymous poem "Should You Go First."

HAWK CHALK VOL. XXI, NO. 2   August, 1982

of the braiding. The knotted button is in the slotted end of the leash. The leash is attached to the swivel by putting the slotted end of the leash through the swivel and then running the whole leash through the slot (see Figure E). Even when the leash is pulled tight, the button is positioned for easy access and removal of the leash (see Figure F).

Any additional information may be obtained by personal correspondence.*

* Footnote -- those who would rather buy than make their equipment may purchase the anklets for $2 a pair and the leashes for $4 each.

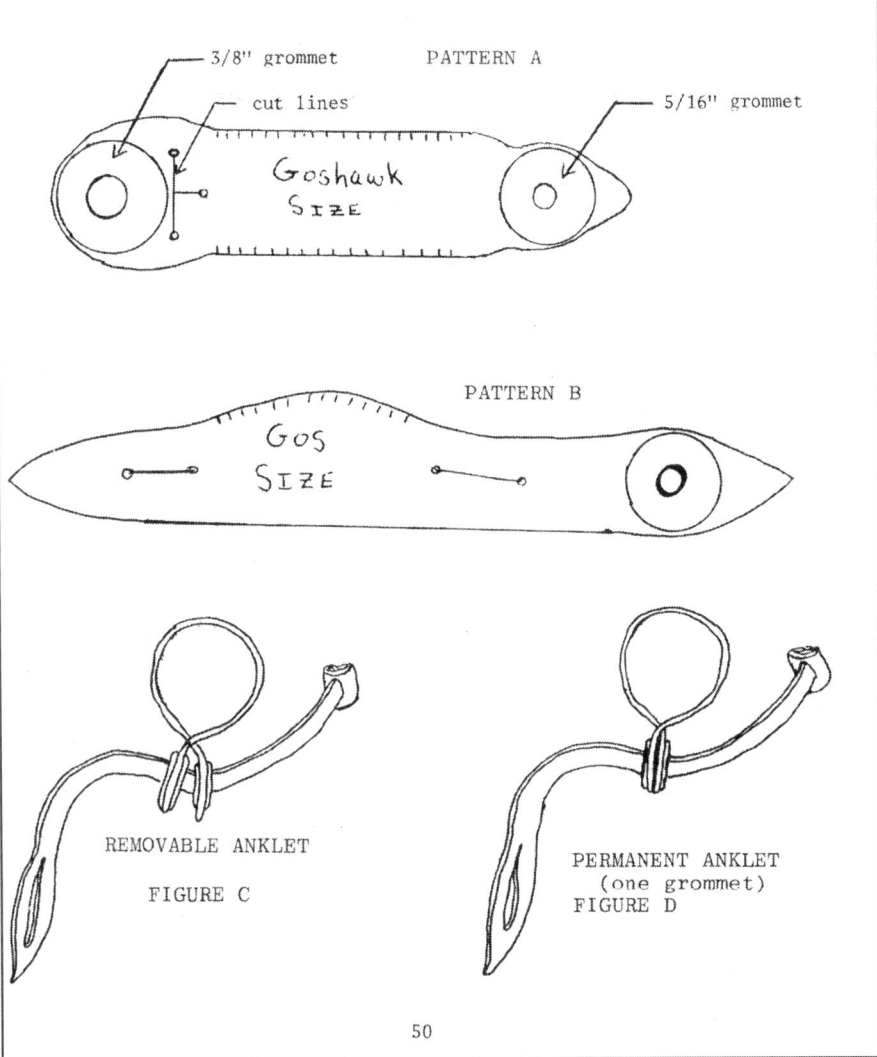

This August 1982 *Hawk Chalk* graphic illustrated my article on the creation of removable anklets that inspired the removable anklets made by falconers all over the world and sold in almost every falconry catalogue.

Chapter 13
Removable Anklets Invented

In 2008 while talking about anklet construction, I mentioned in passing that I had created the removable anklet in the early 1980s.

Joe Ballone looked at me as if I had three heads.

As soon as he got home to Marquette, Michigan, he searched his copy of *Falconry Equipment: A Guide to and and Using Falconry Gear* by Bryan A. Kimsey. Therein he found my name referenced in the anklet section.

The August 1982 NAFA *Hawk Chalk* published my article, "Of Anklet and Leashes." In it I detailed two new designs for removable anklets, one — an adaptation of the classic jess — was a complete failure (see Pattern B).

However, the other was a startling success. It is now used by falconers — and rehabbers — all over the world. Anklets modeled after this design (see Pattern A) are sold in almost every falconer equipment catalogue today.

Obviously, I was surprised that my little anklet design found such a wide acceptance.

Falconers are a very resourceful lot and are prone to adapting and improving patterns to suit their needs. Thus, austringers chase squirrels with created removable "chaps" to protect their hawks from the dangerous and nasty bites. Some falconers make the removable anklets without the grommets, while countless others have changed the shape (see samples on following pages).

The Original Removable Anklet

The original removable pattern was created to make jessing a hawk or falcon easier. This is especially helpful when trapping raptors, such

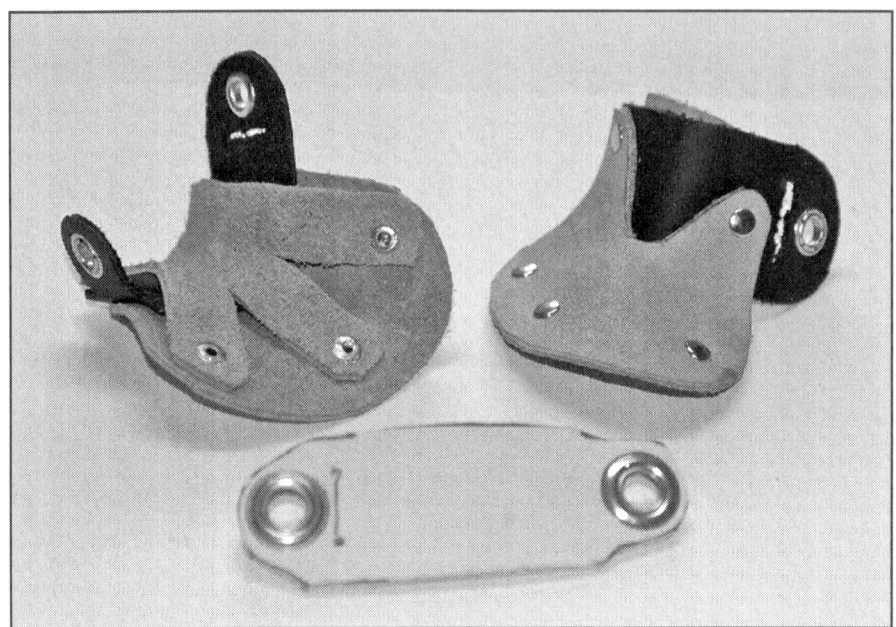

These removable squirrel chaps were made by Michigan falconer Mike Evans of Sturgis. As an avid squirrel hawker, Mike wants as much protection as possible for his hawks. The bottom anklet is my basic design for a female Harris Hawk.

as red-tailed hawks, for use in falconry. Raptor rehabilitators find removable jesses convenient when the birds will only be kept in captivity until they are well enough for release back into the wild. After some practice an anklet can be removed or applied with one hand.

Other falconers keep two or three pairs of anklets. While one pair is in use on the raptor, the others are soaking. This method keeps the anklets in good condition.

Making a Removable Anklet

• Materials needed: Two 3/8" grommets; two 5/16" grommets; two pieces of leather cut to Pattern A. Trial and error will make the needed adjustments as to the specific size needed for your hawk. For smaller birds, one will need to experiment with different sized grommets.

Instructions:

• Trace Pattern A on leather and cut leather to pattern,
• Punch holes for the grommets and set grommets,
• Punch the three small holes next to the 3/8" grommet, then connect the holes by cutting them as shown,
• Place around the hawk's leg and insert the 5/16" grommet through the cut, and then line up the grommets,

• Place your jess through both the grommets. This will keep the anklet from enclosing or expanding (see Figure C).

In 1982, Harry McElroy suggested that this anklet style could be used as a permanent anklet also. This would be done by using the same pattern and by putting the grommet through both thicknesses of leather just as it is done in the Aylmeri anklet (see Figure D).

Nylon Leash Button

The 1982 article also included a little addition for flat, braided nylon leashes. A "nylon button" was suggested to make the leash easier to remove from the swivel by giving the falconer something to grip and pull on. The button never wears out, and as it is part of the braiding. The knotted button is in the slotted end of the leash. The leash was attached to the swivel by putting the slotted end of the leash through the swivel and then running the whole leash through the slot. Even when the leash was pulled tight, the button was easy to access and removal of the leash (see the graphic on Page 102.)

These grommetless jesses were made by Michigan falconer Kory Koch of Mt. Pleasant.

Navarre, a captive-bred male Harris hawk, awaits his chance to fly at both fur and feather.

Chapter 14
Navarre: A Coach's Delight

It was an Indian Summer day.

One of those warm fall days that awakens a joy in every hunter. A calm southwest breeze drifted across one of the few remaining feral fields in northern Indiana. The cover was almost waist high. Small clumps of trees dotted the field. Thick bushes of multiflora rose, and a row of trees fenced every side except along the road.

"That field is the morning feeding ground for the pheasant," Ray Murawski affirmed as he pointed at a small field across the road. "I see them here every morning as I drive to work at 7:30."

Ray was full of confidence.

It was 7:24 a.m.

I had seen confidence in others before. I had also been totally disappointed. Others had promised "a pheasant under every bush" when a child of six could tell there was not a head of game within ten miles of the place. But today was different. I trusted Ray. He was a good friend and a great goshawker.

Today I will be surprised if I am disappointed, I thought.

It was opening day of pheasant season, a day to test ourselves against a worthy opponent. I left the house at 5:07 a.m. to meet Ray at 6 a.m. He was ready to see if this young Harris hawk could live up to his reputation.

We had already hunted starlings that morning. "Navarre," my immature male Harris hawk, had taken two. I wanted to give Ray a good introduction to Harris hawking. He had flown passage goshawks successfully at pheasant for several years. All morning we had shared in the good-natured ribbing that comes when two close friends respect each others accomplishments.

After the first starling was caught, Ray was eager to get to the pheasant field. It had taken a lot of slips at this quarry to catch the first one. He thought that Navarre would soon lose his edge for the pheasant hunt. I could see him wondering as I fed Navarre his reward for the first kill.

"It's alright Ray, he is a Harris hawk," I said as we continued to hunt. Navarre caught his second starling on the very next slip. With that, I conceded and we headed to the pheasant field. Navarre — a 23-ounce (650 gram) hawk — was six months old. After catching the starlings, I knew a new test was before him.

A New Test

Pheasant.

Starlings were the scrimmage in preparation for the "big game." This is not to say that starling flights are not exciting or hard. They are both. But they are difficult to a different degree. The value of a flight is often determined not by the table offering, but by how difficult it is for the raptor to catch that quarry. I do not know anyone who hunts starlings for table food. It's like Olympic diving where every dive is assigned a degree of difficulty, which is multiplied by the score on the quality of the dive. For each raptor every quarry has its own degree of difficulty. For the tiny, sharp-shinned hawk a sparrow is an "easy" quarry. For the Harris it is a very tough quarry. A cottontail may become routine for a Harris but may be impossible for a sharp-shinned hawk. Therefore just as a coach recruits players for specific tasks on his team, falconers select raptors based upon their ability to catch the available quarry.

Navarre was just over two months old when he came to me. From that moment I set out to condition him like a coach would an athlete. He had the natural ability and I was responsible for his physical conditioning, his self confidence and to instill desire.

"Today we shall see if I have instilled desire," I said quietly as I looked into his eyes.

Navarre moved eagerly on the glove. His leg bells rang loudly in the small confines of the truck. We were ready and waiting for the pheasant.

It was 7:37 a.m.

The pheasant were late.

I started ribbing Ray, mumbling about a wild goose chase.

"Maybe we could find a wild goose if the pheasant don't. . ."

My voice faded as first pheasant walked out of the grass onto the road.

"They are coming out the wrong way," Ray said.

They were leaving the small field we expected them to enter. I had planned our attack based on the wind and the small field. No coach likes to have the arena changed at the last minute.

"They must have crossed earlier this morning," Ray added.

"They're here, now it is up to him." I looked at Navarre, stroking his tail with my right hand.

We sat silently as several pheasant crossed the road. Our opponents had come. Were we ready? I knew what it must feel like for a basketball coach to watch the other team warm up before their first game. My hours of study, Navarre's months of conditioning and the endless training had all come down to these few minutes. Then I realized that I was not in control. I could only stand on the sidelines, watch and yell my encouragement. It was up to him.

We had no dog.

"What an edge a dog would be," I said. "It would be an edge on the opponent's home field."

Slowly we opened the doors. The game had begun. Ray circled out in front of the pheasant and cut across the field, left to right. He hoped to keep the pheasant from running into the thick, tall cover where they could just walk away undetected.

"Darn, why don't I have a dog?" I muttered to myself.

Holding Navarre on the glove, I started a crossing pattern like a dog, first right, then left.

Then right again.

Nothing. . .

"Where had they gone?"

Instinctively, I raised Navarre as high as I could on my left hand.

"A little more wind now," I noted trying to envision the pheasant flying downwind.

Ten minutes. Still nothing.

"Do you think they are already beyond you, Ray?" I asked loudly.

Ray turned to answer.

There was no warning.

A rooster pheasant launched out of the grass with a cackle only a few feet away. Navarre was off at the whir of the pheasant like a sprinter at the starter's gun. They flew toward Ray, flying downwind climbing as they went.

They were only ten yards from Ray when Navarre closed the gap to just a few inches.

I was running, cheering and yelling. More pheasant flushed as I rumbled through the cover.

Ray just stood there, smiling. The pheasant dodged left, dropping a little. Navarre turned sharply, swinging his feet up and powered into it. They tumbled from the air almost at Ray's feet. We celebrated like two teenagers after the winning of a state championship. I praised him for his study of pheasant habitat and he praised my coaching success. We relived the exciting moments with several exclamations that began with "Did you see. . .?" "Wasn't that a. . . ?"

"Classic. Eh, Ray?" I said. "Off the glove, on the rise and in the bag!"

"Not bad for a Harris hawk," I commented with a crooked smile.

"My goshawk would be done now," Ray said.

Navarre mantled over the pheasant and looked at me over his shoulder. I knew he was not done. From our many hunts together in the summer, I saw he was eager to continue. We had a oneness that came from our struggle to succeed.

The Bond

Oneness is a mystical union between two souls. The ancient Hebrews used the word "soul" to mean anything that breathed air or anything that was animated. To them man can have oneness with an animal. After all "man's best friend" — the dog — is not human! Falconry is a field sport that allows us to develop a oneness with a wild animal to the point where we strive together for a common goal. Falconry is not like a zoo. Each time we go afield, the raptor is released. It only returns if it decides to fly back. In falconry, hawks and falcons are not kept beyond their desire to stay with us.

Navarre came quickly off the pheasant to the fist.

The hunt continued, but the pheasant were gone.

We made several ever-widening circles around the kill sight. Navarre came and went between the fist and the trees as his curiosity guided him. The wind picked up even more.

"Maybe they crossed back... " Ray said gesturing toward the small field across the road.

"If they have they will be easier to locate," I deduced from its limited area. "I wish I had a dog!"

We circled wide upwind of the small field. A couple of pheasant flew while Navarre was out of position. He had no chance at them. After the chase he took a stand on a power pole, so we worked the field beneath him. When we were halfway across the field, we paused to call Navarre closer.

Just as Navarre hit the fist, Ray bolted a pheasant that crossed right to left 20 yards in front of us. Navarre's bells rang briskly as he cut the corner and pulled in behind him. The pheasant banked sharply to the left. Navarre's tail shifted and a yellow foot shot out. When his left foot hit, it swung his whole body around so that he could grab the cock with his other foot.

Pheasant feathers muffled his bells.

They tumbled to the ground, which reminded me of an ancient Chinese proverb, "You can tie two birds together and though they have four wings, they cannot fly."

"Two pheasant and two starlings," Ray smiled. "What more can you ask for?"

"Nothing," he was sure I would respond.

Navarre's crop was quite full from his reward on four catches.

"Rabbit. . ." I said.

"Rabbit? Will he still hunt?"

"Of course, he's a Harris hawk, remember?" I said as Navarre jumped off the pheasant to a small reward on the glove.

"This used to be a good rabbit and pheasant field before all this construction began," Ray said as we drove into a small field. "There's even a small marsh, if they haven't filled it in."

"It doesn't look like pheasant habitat now," I lamented.

"But it may have a rabbit or two," Ray added.

We worked the field and bumped one rabbit which got quickly to cover. On Ray's reflush it ran upwind. The wind was quite still by then. Navarre flew hard upwind and over came the rabbit which turned back toward the cover. Navarre pitched up into the wind, looking over his shoulder for the fleeing quarry. He went into a rolling stoop and was halfway down when the rabbit cut back upwind. Navarre was pumping in his stoop, twisting as he corkscrewed down onto the rabbit. How he got his feet in front of him I'll never know, but he grabbed the cottontail by the head.

It was over.

A Full Gorge

"We're done now. He deserves a full gorge," I said as we left him to eat his fill on the rabbit.

We walked back to check the marsh.

"Ducks!" I cried out.

"I see them," Ray said of the 20-plus teal and woodies.

"Ducks. . ." I muttered as I turned intently and started walking back.

"Where are you going?"

"The hawk "

"He's not done hunting yet?" Ray quizzed. "He must have a full gorge by now."

Walking briskly I looked back over my shoulder and smiled.

"I know. . ." Ray continued. "He's a Harris hawk, but on a full crop?"

A New Challenge

Navarre stepped casually off the rabbit onto the glove. I stood up slipping the rabbit in with the four birds. Then we were off to a new challenge.

Ducks.

"You're not. . ." Ray said, standing where I left him.

"I won't send him. I just won't stop him," I said.

"Will he come back?"

"Oh, yes. . . A Harris hawk you know," I replied.

It's a little risky, I thought, but he won't leave the fist. He's never seen a duck before. He isn't even hungry.

"Now, how do we get the ducks off the water?" I asked.

Ray yelled.

A few flew off the water. Navarre was off like a shot. The ducks quickly dove back into the water and swam into some thick brush. Navarre pitched up and flew into the trees over the ducks.

"Navarre! Come here Squirt!" I said, lifting my glove.

"Navarre. . ."

He usually returned without a moments hesitation but he didn't respond.

My braggart courage, I thought. *What a fool I can be. I should have never risked it.*

I called. He sat.

I whistled. He only looked.

My watch read 9:45 a.m.

"If he doesn't come down, he'll fly free all day," I said. "He could become lost 60 miles from home."

Ray heard my anxiety building.

"Don't worry. He's a Harris hawk. Remember?" he said with a weak smile.

I slowly shook my head.

"Maybe, he'll come if we flush another rabbit," I suggested. This creative effort seemed to calm my anxiety a little.

"Navarre. . ."

We began walking through some poor cover. We both knew it held no rabbits.

Then came the sweetest music this side heaven: The sound of bells.

Falconry bells.

We both stopped. Ray turned to look, I listened.

Looking straight ahead, I raised my gloved fist. Hearing the bells come closer I casually walked forward, then I heard the solid ring of a hawk hitting the glove.

It was Navarre — a coach's delight.

A falconry T-shirt designed by the author.

My passage Harris hawk was loaned for breeding to Tom and Jennifer Coulson of Louisiana and was lost in hurricane Katrina in 2005.

Chapter 15
Hawking Kearney
A Falconer's Memories of the 1986 NAFA Meet

After church on Sunday morning, Rick Wenneborg — a fellow falconer/preacher from Illinois — and I quizzed some of the local folks in Kearney, Nebraska about where to find quarry. The local preacher, who had planned to hunt at his best pheasant spot Monday, promised to take us there instead.

Everyone mentioned "north" when they spoke quarry, so we went north Sunday afternoon.

Finding a few likely spots, such as abandoned farm sites, we stopped to ask for permission. A farmer's son pointed out four fields to hunt. In the first field we found nothing. In the second field we saw one cottontail disappear quickly down a hole. The third field held one rabbit, which disappeared into a wood pile. By the fourth field — thinking there must be a one-rabbit-per-field quota — we were set to leave as soon as the rabbit escaped under an old farm house. We began to sense our knowledge of rabbit habitat might not match Nebraska terrain.

Going South

At the Ramada Inn that evening, we listened to jubilant reports of white-tailed jackrabbits "bigger than dogs," black-tail jacks, cottontails and quail all south of town. I located the Kentucky crew — Keith Hix and Dave Campbell — and Bill and Mary Shank from Ohio. We made plans for Monday morning — to go south.

We found a likely spot — a woodlot with a creek running through it. The owner not only told us where to find game but how to get there. He added that he had two bedrooms that we could have used for the week and he would have fed us too. Now that was a great Nebraska welcome.

We flew the Harris hawks first. Keith flew his first-year female, "Cody;" Bill his first-year, "Lady;" Rick his intermewed female, "Jae Tsing" (Chinese for "smart and faster"); and I had my cast of inter-mewed "Ladyhawke" and immature Navarre. Hatched in February 1986, Navarre was trying to make a name for himself so I would quit calling him "Sarah's brother."

In the first field, we flushed plenty of cottontails in some 6-foot weeds, and Cody caught three. Lady and Jae took one each. We flushed some quail, had a few nice flights but nabbed none. Navarre pulled fur on a couple of rabbits but couldn't hang on.

Fox Squirrel Frenzy

A half-dozen times we were prepared to leave that field, but kept flushing rabbit at the corner fence and ended up back in the field. In a nearby woodlot, Lady stooped down a tree trunk and tried to bind to a fox squirrel. It ran into a scrap pile as the hawks took their stations above. With some beating, the squirrel finally ran out. The next moment was one giant blur of black feathers and yellow feet. One of the hawks hit from the left, and as I ran over I saw one mature tail-feather in the midst of 11 immature feathers.

"Navarre!" I yelled in panic.

I try to avoid squirrels while flying Harris hawks, especially chasing huge fox squirrels with a 22-ounce (620-gram) tiercel. I dove head-first and grabbed at the squirrel's head. Thankfully Navarre was not bitten and I hoped he'd never get an opportunity to catch another.

Later we spotted another fox squirrel, and the two intermewed females were the most adamant in the chase. They were not experi-enced in squirrel hawking and missed as it bridged from the top of one tree to another. But they did panic the squirrel as it bolted to an old leaf nest that had only the base left.

It was a sitting duck, as Jae Tsing was on it in a flash. The squirrel screamed that raspy growl, which told us she didn't have a command-ing hold. It was squirming around on the nest and managed to pull most of it body over the nest edge. Then suddenly it was falling to the ground at our feet. It fell 35 feet and literally hit the ground running. Each of the females took shots at it as it darted around and through the brush. Just as it cleared the brush a hawk grabbed him by the rear end.

That's dangerous. It's the wrong end! I thought. Seeing the one mature tail feather I realized it was Navarre again.

Dave was closer and — knowing my fears — quickly intervened.

Thank you, Dave!" I said relieved, as we marveled at the size of the huge buck squirrel.

We searched Navarre for wounds and found none. However later in the week we found a scratch on the killing talon on his right foot. We were unsure if it was the squirrel encounter or occured from the times Jae Tsing attacked him.

Honest Nebraska Folks

We hunted pheasant with the local preacher in another small woods on Monday afternoon. We went 35 miles northwest, were given permission by a 70-year-young farmer and were watched from a pickup by an elderly couple. Hawking in a draw with thick brush, we didn't flush any pheasant but put up some cottontails.

The heavy cover made it tough to catch them. The farmer rolled down his window and commented that he wasn't very impressed with the hawks' performance.

That's honest Nebraska folks for you!

Just then shouts of "Ho... Ho!" rang out as a rabbit bolted. Running into a small opening, it was caught by Lady with great style and a tumbling slide.

I smiled at the farmer and asked, "Is that any better?"

The preacher took us to a second field where we exercised some pheasant with Dave's intermixed female goshawk. These sure were not Indiana pheasant; these birds were used to flying miles before landing. One cock flew off and landed in the top of a distant tree. When we got too close for his approval, he promptly flew to the next county.

On Tuesday, our same crew plus Michigan falconers Joe Vorro and Everet Horton left early for a pasture where two jackrabbits had been seen. Soon after we formed a rough line, the first jack bolted in the center of our line. It ran upwind toward a fence — the only cover within a mile. The hawks pursued and disappeared over the rolling terrain. Climbing the hill, we saw Jae stoop at the foot of the fence, grabbing the jack by the head. A successful conclusion.

A Sure Catch

Next we bumped a cottontail near some scrap metal, but it escaped under an overturned watering tank. Being the sporting gentlemen we were, we positioned ourselves around the tank as Dave turn it over.

With no cover, where could it run? A sure catch?

Wrong!

Cottontails do not cotton to getting caught. After this one outran, out-dodged and out-witted all its pursuers — raptor and human — it simply jogged off upwind. The humbled crew combed the rest of the field and flushed one more jackrabbit and a cottontail. The last was caught by Jae after a nice flight downwind, and of course, toward a fence.

In the field across the road, our line of beaters flushed a jack. All the hawks bolted off at the same time with Navarre the first to reach the rabbit. As he footed the jackrabbit, it sprang into the air in an effort to escape. It probably would have except at the peak of his leap, it was greeted by two immature Harris hawks. The ladies proved that behind every good man is a great woman — or two. It appeared as it jumped right into their feet.

When I found the tiny Navarre on the bottom of 10 pounds of jackrabbit and Harris hawk, I thought this might not be the best way to introduce a young bird to jack hawking. I wondered if he'd ever chase another.

High Hopes, High Winds

After lunch we drove west, but the wind kicked up as high as 45 mph. A gas station attendant directed us to a thickly brushed feral field surrounded by cultivated fields, where we flushed 12 jacks and six pheasant. But the high winds made catching them a nearly impossible proposition. We promised ourselves to return early the next day.

At dawn on Wednesday, we were back and flew Steve Heying's peregrine/prairie "Max" at pheasant. We couldn't seem to get the right time. The pheasant flushed when Max was out of position. Then we pursued jack slips for Dave's goshawk. We got several slips, but the gos was not very thrilled with all the company.

When the Harris hawks flew, we had several unsuccessful flights on jackrabbits that ran upwind across an open field and escaped. One finally bolted downwind. Navarre almost caught up to it, then for 35 to 40 yards followed its every move and shift, as tiercels do best. Although he missed, it was a classic heat-seeking missile flight. I was pleased he still chased jacks.

Bill Shank carried Lady and I took Narvarre and worked a ditchline downwind of Joe Vorro and Ladyhawke, Keith Hix and Cody, and Rick Wenneborg and Jae. Bill and I tried to flush a jack toward them. As we hoped, the next jackrabbit bolted upwind toward the others. With Navarre dogging it — just like the previous jack — he made it lose speed by turning it several times.

Then Jae swept in with a great show of power and grandeur and rolled the jack. It was the prettiest cast flights of the whole meet.

On Thanksgiving Day, we concentrated on hawking pheasant in a spot west of Kearney shown to us by a friendly school principal. We met him in the morning at his mother-in-law's home. Emma Monter, in her 70s, went into the field to see the birds fly and beat the bush with us. She'll wear out before she rusts out, we said. She told us her brother used to run a trapline in the old days. He would be gone for days at a time, walking miles home with several coyotes on his back.

Two Great Ladies

During that time Mary Shank went off with her red-tailed hawk. She caught three rabbits with her female red-tail. Bill is lucky to have two very nice ladies.

Steve flew Max and his 7-year-old tiercel prairie falcon, "Papi," together at pheasant. Max didn't like the idea, so Steve put Papi up and we began working the cornfield toward the draw. Steve's dog worked the fence row and we walked in a line. The prairie was behind us when the dog went on point by a plum thicket. The cock flushed prematurely and the chase was on. The falcon was about 350 feet up.

The 16-ounce tiercel flew straight across the sky until he was over the fleeing pheasant and then stooped on him. Unfortunately the actual strike was obscured by the plum thicket and rolling hills. The tiercel struck the cock, but it broke free and flew to cover, leaving a trace of feathers to mark the point of confrontation.

Then the Harris hawks had a try at what may have been the same pheasant — they didn't stand a chance. Navarre had caught two Indiana pheasants, both off the glove on the rise, but the Nebraska pheasants were from a different genetic stock. Jae did show the rabbits some sport and caught one in the plum thicket.

Cody's Day

On Friday, we were in Overton with the jacks we'd been exercising. Cody grabbed several jacks but did not catch any.

Friday was her day.

She caught one in thick cover, but when Keith got there somehow in all the confusion the jack broke free and bolted. Later, we worked a brush-line between two cultivated fields and flushed a jack, which — not surprisedly — ran upwind. Jae and Cody chased it as it circled back into cover. They were almost side by side, flying 30 feet high when they got to the rabbit. Cody banked left, rolled and stooped like a fighter jet. Instantly Jae followed her in the same maneuver. Everyone heard the growl as Cody smacked the critter.

Not to be outdone, Jae caught a jack from a phone pole as we worked the rest of the brush. Navarre grabbed another jackrabbit but was bucked off when Cody and Ladyhawke didn't arrive in time.

People were the key to the success of the Meet, but some hawks also became personified at the Meet. That week Rick's Jae and Keith's Cody etched a place in my memory.

For me the success of the NAFA Meet had more to do with people and hawks than quarry and weather.

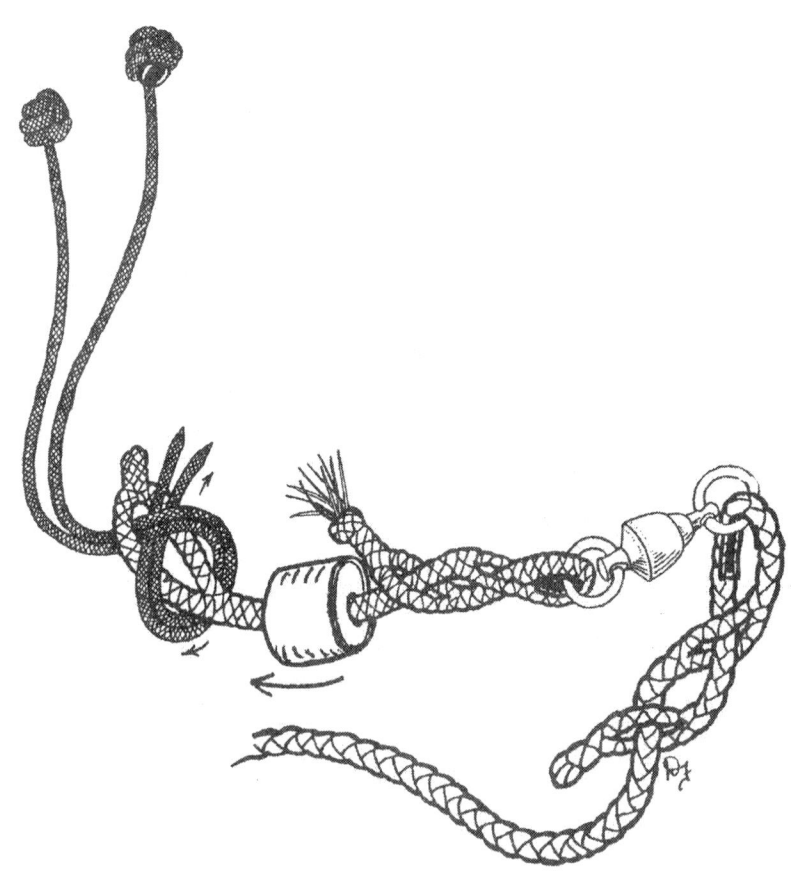

This graphic was created by my (now deceased) brother Don Filkins for an article on arab jesses in a *Hawk Chalk*.

A man watches at close range, as a passage red-tailed hawk chases a cottontail at a Michigan Hawking Club Meet.

Joe Ballone, of Marquette, Michigan, holds his 2010 trapped red-tail, Ember, and a black squirrel. Ember caught the squirrel with great style as the last light of day disappeared in Sault Ste. Marie, Michigan.

Chapter 16
Quest for The Black One

Joe Ballone's red-tails and my Harris hawks had caught gray squirrels in the Upper Peninsula of Michigan — "da U.P.," as Yoopers call it. Our hawks had chased black squirrels, tagged them and pulled their tails but never bagged one.

Of course, there is no difference between a gray squirrel and a black squirrel except color. But, as falconers who frequently saw those black critters escape by the length of their fur, catching one became our quest.

Joe's first red-tailed hawk, "Mystic," was an amazing hunter — especially for squirrels. Joe released her after her second season. Her thrilling flights and the black squirrels' narrow escapes only hardened our resolved to catch one.

We dedicated the afternoon of November 20 to our "black" quest. With a higher percentage of black squirrels in the Eastern Upper Peninsula — "da EUP" — Joe and his new passage red-tail, "Ember," visited Sault Ste. Marie.

Ember's Fear

Ember was shy when anyone but Joe was in the field, so Joe had me call her down from a tree a few times when we arrived at an abandoned campground near Lake Superior State University. She seemed to tolerate my presence as she would fly to the glove me to Joe and back.

Ember followed well — another sign of acceptance — then chased the first squirrel hard. She pressured the squirrel to bridge over to another tree then quickly scamper down a fallen tree that rested at a 45-degree angle against its escape tree. Ember bolted down the 45-degree tree and slammed into the gray squirrel as it hit the ground.

Joe ran over, but the squirrel had struggled free leaving Ember with squirrel hair in the snow.

Encouraged by her response with me in the field we went to another squirrel hotspot in a woods near a city playground. As we approached Ember spotted a gray scampering up a huge poplar tree.

The Squirrel Condo

Ember made a pass at it as I saw three holes in the tree. The holes were in a vertical line, three to four feet apart. It looked like a perfect tree condominium. I feared the critter would soon disappear into one of the holes. As Ember marked the squirrel, I saw a squirrel nose poke out of the top hole. At the same time, Joe started beating on the tree with his hands, the gray popped out of the top hole.

Then a second one climbed out of the middle hole. And a third gray darted out of the top hole. They bailed out of the holes like someone had just triggered a fire alarm.

Instantly, the tree was swarming with squirrels.

Ember took shots at the squirrels. The condo trio were adults, and the original one was a yearling. Ember isolated the younger one after some chases through the treetops before it scrambled to the top of a thinner tree and froze.

Once the trio realized that the tree was not falling down and saw the danger of staying exposed to a red-tailed hawk, they disappeared one by one back into the poplar condominium.

The younger squirrel stayed froze in the crotch of the tree and wouldn't move.

Ember lost sight of the squirrel. All the shaking of the tree throwing sticks and snowballs at the squirrel did not frighten it.

Finally, Joe resorted to shooting marbles at it with a slingshot. But the dime-store marbles were not designed for shooting, so they went any direction but straight. None flew near the frozen squirrel.

Next he tried some lead shot that I just happened to have in my jacket pocket. It was small and had little effect on the tree critter.

Straight Shooting

So we changed hawks. I guarded the tree as Joe took Ember back and he watched the squirrel as I took out my intermewed Harris hawk, Sadie.

Again we tried to flush the statue squirrel, to no avail. Sadie could not figure out what all the yelling, tree slapping and stick throwing was about.

From her high perch at the top of a tree, Sadie spotted a squirrel

100 yards to the west. As I tracked her, I could hear her bells as she chased a squirrel out of a tree then under some low cedar trees another 30 yards further. When I arrived, Sadie was in a tall white pine tree. She whined to tell me she sees the quarry. It was a cat-and-mouse game where Sadie would ladder up the heavily branched tree until the climber panicked and darted down the tree several feet. Sadie charged after it and got hung up on the branches. I was hoping she would not catch this bushy-tail, because she would likely get caught up on the branches and be at a disadvantage for the fight.

Fortunately, I was able to call her down and return to the hunt for the frozen statue.

As I arrived at the condo tree, I realized I had purchased some pricey, white marbles — those specifically for slingshots.

"Joe, you're our only hope," I told him as he came back from retrieving the white straight shooters from the vehicle. "If we're going to get that critter, you're going to have to hit it."

Joe zeroed in on our target. He pelted the area around the squirrel with white round missiles. One of Joe's sniper shots glanced off the frozen statue.

It moved six inches around the trunk then slipped right back into the crouch. It was careful enough to do so when Sadie could not see it. Finally Sadie flew off 30 yards to check out a possible squirrel sighting. I started calling her back.

Joe kept flinging missiles as Sadie was flying back. While she was in the air, Joe hit the squirrel square enough to knock it from the tree. It fell from the tree like a clown shot out of a cannon and wildly threw its arms in every direction. Its antics didn't change its fall.

The instant it hit the snow, Sadie greeted her.

The battle was over.

It was gray.

The Quest Continued

Our quest for a black beast led to my main squirrel spot near a local gravel pit. As we searched from the road, the short November day was dwindling away. Though many blacks lived in that woods, none were sighted. Mystic had caught two squirrels a day from there on two other hunts, but no blacks flushed.

We considered flying there on speculation, but decided to hunt again at the original woods near the university.

With fading light we worked the other sections of that woods. As we had seen the previous season, very fresh squirrel tracks were everywhere in the new snow.

But no squirrels moved.

As the daylight grew dimmer, we walked toward the last of woods — still no squirrel sighting.

At seemingly the last moment, the woods were alive with bushy-tails. A black squirrel and two or three gray squirrels — it was hard to tell just how many climbers were afoot with all the action happening simultaneously. Squirrels danced through the trees as Ember put in two hard strikes at a gray. From where I was, it looked like the black, but Joe — who was closer to the action — later confirmed that it was a gray.

The gray escaped but the black one was still in a tree. Ember pressured it out of a tree as it crossed a lane the took refuge in larger tree. As had happened at the playground woods, this quarry tried to freeze into a fur-covered statue. Fearing Ember would be shy and not wanting anything to mess up this chance for a black one, I stood off at a distance.

Ember Still Feared Me

Joe shot white marbles at it to scare it into action. He got it to move and even grazed it a couple times. But Ember would not chase it. Joe noticed that she kept looking back and forth between me and the squirrel. When the squirrel moved, she would look to see where I was then stay in her tree.

So I moved farther away to the vehicle that was 50 yards down the lane. As soon as I was away and the black one moved, Ember charged after it instantly and with intent to do bodily harm.

From my location I could still see the action with the sunset behind the leafless trees, red-tail, squirrel and Joe. Standing there, I thought how this would be the perfect ending if Ember could only catch this black critter.

But she didn't have much time. Night was falling like a curtain.

Joe's shot grazed it again and the climber bridged over to another tree, as Ember made chase. However, in its hurry the squirrel lost its hold and fell toward the ground. As I saw the whole chase silhouetted against the sunset, I thought Ember would make quick work of this falling squirrel.

As the black one fell it grabbed a small branch bending it like a bow. The squirrel's decent then stopped as the power of the limb flung the critter skyward. As quick as it fell, it was tossed back on a small limb and darted toward the trunk.

With Ember pursuing, it climbed up the tree then launched another escape by bridging to a larger tree. It made it over the bridge. As it ran down a larger branch, Ember pursued it by flying down the limb with her wings beating on either side of the branch and her breast almost rubbing the bark. When the black squirrel got to the crutch of the tree and tried to escape around the trunk, Ember slammed into it. Moments later they were dropping to the ground. I could not tell what had happened until I heard Joe yell.

"Did she get it?" I asked loudly.

"Yes, she did!"

The celebration was on.

Photos were taken.

Another great day of hawking ended the quest for the black one.

During a spring migration a trio of sharp-shinned hawks fly across the dunes at White Fish Point along Michigan's Lake Superior shoreline.

Mike Jones, of South Bend, Indiana, holds a northern harrier just before its release. Mike first trapped birds of prey at Whitefish Point in 1963. In 1973, Mike obtained his own USFWS banding permit under the Kellogg Bird Sanctuary, and he has been banding at Whitefish Point every year since.

Chapter 17
Fishing The Sky

From a blind we watched seven hawks soaring in the windy skies over the dunes of Whitefish Point, when suddenly one hawk folded its wings and dropped from the sky. The hawk was diving toward us, and the lure bird near the bow net was flapping to the rhythm of Mike Jones' tugs. The lure's strings were attached to a nearby pole and ran to the blind. The hawk kept descending and soon grabbed the starling on the line. Mike pulled the starling with the sharp-shinned hawk to the bow-net.

With a tug on the bow's trigger string, the small hawk was captured.

Jones retrieved the unharmed sharp-shin from the net then returned to the blind. With masterful hands that had performed the task thousands of times, he selected a metal band and placed it on the bird's leg. He recorded all the data of the banding on his official log sheet — including the date, time, location, and the bird's species, age and sex — then he slipped his hand out the door and released the hawk. It disappeared into the woods to continue its journey north across Lake Superior to its nesting area in Canada.

Watching the sky for soaring hawks then trying to lure them earthward feels like fishing: Fishing the sky.

Mike is a master of sky fishing.

Mike, from South Bend, Indiana, has been a falconer since 1963 and master bird bander for decades. He bands raptors for the U.S. Fish and Wildlife Service (USFWS) and first trapped migrant birds of prey at Whitefish Point in 1963 as an assistant to a bird bander. In 1973 Mike obtained his own USFWS banding permit under the

Kellogg Bird Sanctuary, and he has been banding every year since at Whitefish Point in the Upper Peninsula of Michigan.

"Whitefish Point, as far as I know, is the best spring hawk banding location there is," Mike said while we sat in his blind waiting for another visitor from the sky. "The migrating hawks travel up both sides of Lake Michigan then enter the Upper Peninsula, where they run into Lake Superior and look for a place to jump across to Canada. Whitefish Point is like a north-pointing funnel that collects the hawks before they cross over."

For decades banders and bird watchers have gathered in late April and early May to observe this migration unique to the Eastern Upper Peninsula. Banders gather on the dunes in a close-knit matrix of blinds and nets.

Birdwatchers view the migrant raptors from the elevated viewing platform behind the Whitefish Point Shipwreck Museum near the Lake Superior shore. From the platform, birdwatchers overlook the dunes where the hawks, falcons, eagles and owls are lured out of the sky into nets of banders.

While we visited, an immature female goshawk stooped at the lure bird then sat in a snag some 25 yards from the blind. It had evaded the mist nets. Mike pulled the lines and the starling flapped but to no avail. The goshawk turned and darted off over the dune through the trees.

"That was a $100 bird," Mike said. "Tim Lickly and I have a $100 bet on the guy who traps the first goshawk when we are both here. He caught one before I was up here, and I caught one when he was down-state, but that one would be the $100 bird. We don't get many goshawks each year."

Tim and his wife, Lori, from the Clare, Michigan area, also band hawks at Whitefish each year. Some years ago Tim put up $100 bill for whoever caught the first goshawk. Now the bill passes back and forth depending on who wins each year.

"Tim has had it for the last few years," Mike lamented.

"It's time for us to get it back," Mills said.

The goshawk is a rare but not unusual catch at Whitefish. Mostly the banders catch the smaller sharp-shinned hawks, a few Cooper's hawks, some northern harriers and only a few of the plentiful red-tailed hawks, which are not often lured down. On even more rare occasions they catch merlin or peregrine falcon, and only one golden eagle has ever been trapped at Whitefish Point. Jones caught it on April 27, 2000.

The banders also work after dark to catch owls — such as barred, great gray, long ear and short ear owls — to band them as a part of the USFWS migration data.

While visiting Mike for the day I also walked over to see bird bander Stan Marcus, of Midland. His blind was high on a dune and from
there we watched and netted several sharp-shinned hawks. Most of
the birds we saw did not come into the lure birds but during the day
between the two blinds and the platform I saw 100-plus birds of prey
including red-tailed hawks, which are like miniature eagles.

"There's a red-tail," Stan said looking up through the tiny window
of his camouflaged tent/blind. "When they are overhead the other
hawks are afraid to come down because they fear being attacked by
the red-tail if they land."

Between the four blinds that day, they banded dozens of sharp-
shinned hawks, a couple Cooper's hawks and one marsh hawk.

Not a bad day's fishing.

A Month Each Spring

For decades Mike has spent every day from April 15 to May 15 trapping and banding raptors at Whitefish Point. Clearly his passion for
banding hawks, falcons and owls has not diminished in four decades.

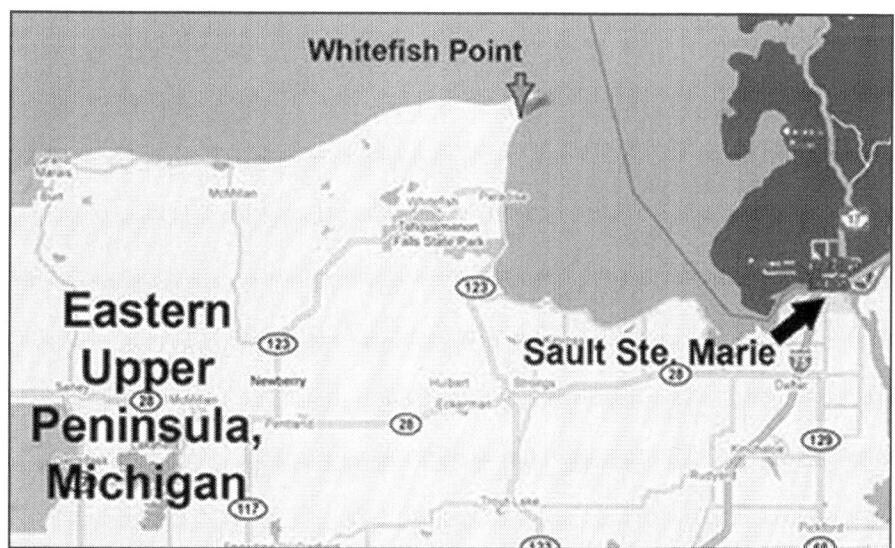

Whitefish Point is touted as the best spring hawk banding site in the United States.
The migrating hawks travel up both sides of Lake Michigan, then enter Michigan's
Upper Peninsula. When they run into Lake Superior they travel along it looking for a
place to "jump across" to Canada. Whitefish Point is like a north-pointing funnel
that collects the hawks before they crossover. For decades banders have gathered
from mid-April to mid-May on the dunes in a close-knit matrix of blinds and nets.

A starling screams as a sharp-shinned hawk nabs the other lure bird.

Mike — a retired M&M candy rep — spends a month in the Upper Peninsula and each fall bands in Wisconsin along the west shore of Lake Michigan.

Some spring trips are slower for banding than others. In 2001 he was a couple of birds short of banding 300 birds at Whitefish.

"Last year, by April 27, I had banded 108 birds. This year by that date I only had 54," Mike said in 2002. "Many hawks may have passed through during an early warm spell. When I got here the weather turned snowy."

By April 30 Mike had caught one goshawk, a red-tail hawk, two harriers, 12 long ear owls, and three kestrel falcons — among a host of sharp-shinned hawks. One bald eagle and a merlin falcon came over on April 20 but neither stooped to the nets, Mike said. But that day he added considerably to his 2002 numbers by banding 28 hawks.

All banders hope to recapture some previously banded hawks to add to the scientific knowledge about raptor migration habits. Details from every bird are uploaded into the USFWS banding database so banders can learn the history of a previously banded hawk.

In the fall of 1985, Mike banded an immature female sharp-shinned hawk during the fall migration in Grafton, Wisconsin. Five years later, in the spring of 1990, he recaptured the same female during the spring migration at Whitefish Point. That is a rare treat — for the same bander to catch a hawk in a different state, in a different season, he said.

Not so unusual is the re-trapping of a bird by different banders at Whitefish Point during the same migration. As Mike banded a hawk on April 30, the radio cracked with the voice of Stan, who asked if Mike had banded a bird with the number 19602. Mike said he had banded that hawk at 4:36 p.m.

Stan re-trapped it at 5:20 p.m. the same day.

On May 4, Mike trapped a sharp-shinned hawk that had been trapped two days prior at Whitefish by Tim. That day, Mike caught 24 hawks and Stan caught 23 — including a harrier — and Tim caught over 50 hawks.

Which bander sees the most hawks is largely dependent on the wind direction, Mike said. That Saturday, Tim's blind was the hot location. In a 20 minute period that afternoon, more than two dozen hawks darted around the lures. At one moment four birds sat in the birch trees and jack pines, while eight more dived and stooped at the lures. Finally, four triggered the nets, while 10 more were soaring in the blue sky.

Mike said that birders, banders and hawks are not his only encounters at Whitefish Point. In the spring of 2001, he had a cow moose stare him down outside his trailer-style blind. Fearing it would run into his nets, Mike tried to scare it in the opposite direction by yelling and charging at it. Instead of fleeing, the moose charged back at him and ran him into his blind to find safety.

The master hawk trapper found himself trapped in his blind by a cow.

2005 "The Worst Season"

April 15 to May 4, 2005 was "the worst banding season," Mike said. It was so slow that he planned to cut short his stay by a week. All that changed on May 5 when the weather warmed and a southwest wind funneled a swarm of hawks, falcons and owls toward Whitefish Point.

It was a very busy day for all the banders. On that Thursday, Mike's one day catch equaled a quarter of his catch from the three previous weeks. He banded some 40 birds that day.

In 2005, Mike caught two birds that he had trapped the year before. On April 25, 2005 he recaptured a sharp-shinned hawk that he first banded as an adult female on April 20, 2004. On May 2, 2005 he trapped another adult female sharpy that was first caught on April 28, 2004.

"And both bands were within three numbers of each other," Mike said with some amazement.

After a very poor start to the season, Mike reported that it turned out to be a record year for him. He broke his previous record — 299 birds in 2004 — by 19 hawks. Mike banded 318 birds.

Jones' Journal Notes

• In the fall of 1973, 36 goshawks were caught.

• October 16, 1983, Mike and a friend set-up the blind and when the friend went to park the car, Mike tested the pigeon lines. He gave them a pull or two when a bird came out of nowhere, grabbing the pigeon. Mike pulled the pigeon over and sprang the bow net. They had their first peregrine of the day. That bird was rewrapped in North Carolina on September 23, 1984.

• October 5, 1986, a passage tiercel peregrine falcon was caught in very poor condition with mud-covered and dull talons.

• October 6, 1986, another peregrine was trapped, banded and released. When he was released he stayed around even though they were outside the blind. Mike pulled the pigeon, and the falcon made 10-12 stoops at it before it left.

• May 26, 1985, an eyass red-tailed hawk was banded in a nest in South Bend, Indiana. On January 5, 1986 it was found dead on a road near Montgomery, Ohio.

• An adult female sharpy banded on May 5, 1979 at Whitefish Point in Michigan was re-trapped on September 23, 1980 in Duluth, Minnesota.

• An adult female sharpy was banded by Mike on May 7, 1980 in upper Michigan was rewrapped May 7, 1984 by Warren Lamb in the same spot.

• An adult female goshawk banded on October 15, 1973 in Duluth was shot on July 20, 1980 in Dawson Creek, British Columbia, Canada. This female was one of 13 goshawks banded on that day. Five were females and only three were passage.

• An adult female goshawk banded on October 16, 1973 in Duluth was retrapped on March 3, 1976 in Meadow Lark, Saskatchewan.

Stan Marcus

Over four decades ago, Stan Marcus ventured north from Midland to Whitefish Point with friends to trap and band migrating hawks.

It was a weekend trip. They slept in a van, got stuck in the sand and trapped a bunch of sharp-shinned hawks. Stan got sick. He was hospitalized with a gall bladder attack.

"We had a lot of fun," Stan, the retired Dow Chemical engineer,

Former NAFA President, Stan Marcus holds a freshly trapped goshawk before its release. Over four decades ago, Stan first came to Whitefish Point with Al Kuntsen, then a Lansing resident and Escanaba native. Stan, of Coleman, Michigan, was also the first president of the North American Peregrine Foundation and is a Master Raptor Bander for the USFWS. The longest "return" Stan has had of his 60 re-trapped hawks, was a sharp-shinned hawk found dead in Nicaragua. It is likely the farthest recapture of any Whitefish Point bird, he said.

recalled while peering out from his camouflaged tent at Whitefish Point 40 years later.

The decades of trapping and that spring's wet, cool weather had not dampened the long-time falconer's excitement of watching another hawk or falcon dive to his lure starling.

"When we first came up to Whitefish Point, we were sub-banders under Lansing resident — and Escanaba native — Al Knutsen," Stan recalled. Not many years later, Stan got his own master banding permit from the USFWS.

Stan's early interest in banding hawks grew from his passion for fal-

Mike Jones bands a sharp-shinned hawk before its release.

conry. As president of the North American Falconers' Association in the early 1970s, Stan worked with the federal government to create national falconry regulations. He was also the first president of the North American Peregrine Foundation, which supported the efforts at Cornell University to produce the first peregrine falcons for reintroduction into the wild.

The first breeding peregrines came from falconers donating their birds to the recovery project, Stan recalled as another red-tailed hawk soared over his blind.

"In the early years, we came up for long weekends," Stan recalled. "We'd go smelt dipping and do all kinds of stuff. Now we don't have nearly the energy we did in those days. Eventually, we went from weekend trips to taking a week or two of vacation to band hawks at Whitefish.

"Since I retired in 1992, I've spent three to four weeks here," Stan added. "As you can guess, the number of birds trapped increased with the time spent."

Through the four decades, Stan has seen several surprising changes in the raptor population he and the others have banded. His first trapping adventures resulted in mostly sharp-shinned hawks, a few northern harriers and red-tailed hawks. Though the small sharp-shinned hawks still make up the vast majority of the banded raptors, other birds of prey have been climbing up the list.

"We are catching more and more broadwing hawks," Stan said. "For decades, we saw many broadwings fly through, but only now are we starting to catch them. Merlin falcons have also been a more frequent capture. After years of not catching any, we began trapping one this year, then two that year. Finally, I trapped nine merlins one spring. That was an environmental indicator that the merlins had come back" (after the ban on the pesticide DTT).

Stan added roughlegged hawks to his list of "only recently trapped," indicating that five were banded one spring.

He has also trapped Cooper's hawks, goshawks, kestrel falcons, and a host of owls — including barred, boreal, great gray, great horned, long ear and short ear. Stan had a golden eagle come into this trapping set, but the huge raptor simply tore up his equipment and left.

The longest "return" Stan has had of his 60 re-trapped hawks, is a sharp-shinned hawk found dead in Nicaragua. It is likely the farthest recapture of any Whitefish Point bird, he said.

One weekend in the 1970s, Stan was thrilled to band 35 birds in three days with his wife's help. In the 1990s while his sub-banders' birds were still reported in his numbers, they trapped around 650 birds one spring migration season. These days, four or five banders setup in a close network of blinds at the Point.

That closeness surely decreases the hawk count of each bander, Stan said. "But it's not as bothersome as one might think," he added of the banders.

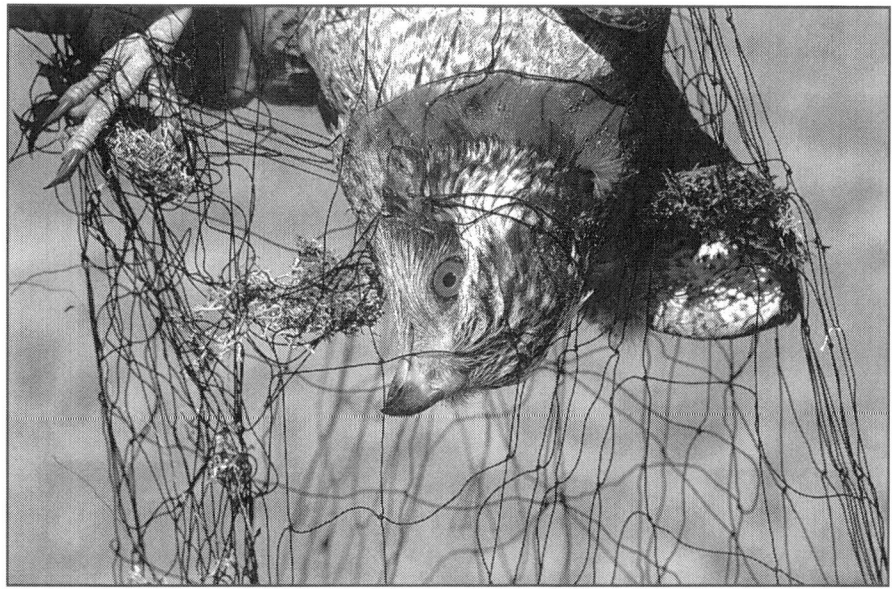

Stan Marcus caught this goshawk in a net then banded and released it.

Lori Lickly bands a hawk while her husband, Tim, holds it on the dunes of Whitefish Point.

Tim and Lori Lickly

With over two decades of banding hawks each spring and over 30 years of marriage, two Dow chemists work together with precision to capture birds of prey at Whitefish Point.

"We rarely miss," Lori Lickly of Clare said of their bird banding teamwork with her husband Tim. "I lure them in, and Tim is the trigger man."

Together, Tim and Lori average some 200 raptors banded each spring from the two blinds they operate. In 2000, they set their personal record with 401 birds banded — which was later broken. They even captured 137 raptors — all sharp-shinned hawks — on one day, said Tim. Another 32 were trapped the next day, making nearly half of their record year's total in just two days. That was a very unusual weekend, Lori said.

In 2003, the outdoor couple had over 350 hawks captured and banded by May 15.

No huge, one-day catch added to that year's total, Tim said. Rather, the increase came from a change in the trapping location for their "second blind." In 2003 long-time friend and banding mentor Stan was unable to band at Whitefish, so Tim and Lori set up both of their blinds on top of the dune. In previous years, their second blind was farther down in the woods. The result has been consistently higher catches of birds of prey.

Stan started the Lickly couple on this banding journey in 1987 when Lori expressed an interest in falconry. When Lori approached Stan, he "strongly suggested" that they come to Whitefish Point for banding that spring, she recalled. They went and soon became caught in the adventure.

"Stan got me hooked," Tim said. "The first year we came up for four days, and by the next year I knew that was too short a time. For me, raptor banding brings my biology background and my love of the outdoors together."

Lori's affection for the outdoors is just as natural.

"She is one of the most avid outdoor women I've ever met," Tim said of her training of golden retrievers, judging field trials and running dogs in field competitions.

Tim does all the equipment maintenance, the blind setup and early season scouting, Lori said, while adding that she waits until the weather warms before making her first spring trip north.

"Hawk banding is an extension of my hunting season," said Lori, an avid duck hunter. "This is really similar to (duck) hunting because you lure the quarry in. But this is nicer because you don't kill the quarry.

"As a couple, we both enjoy being up here and what we do," Lori added. "We work as a team."

Sixteen-week-old Gabi sports her immature plummage. She was bred by Chris Shaw of Eagle, Michigan. She is the daughter of the noted Harris hawk pair "Phil and Trish." Gabi is a small female halfway between the weights of a male and female Harris hawk.

Chapter 18
A Falconry Parable

While hunting, a falconer fell into a pit and couldn't get himself out.

A subjective austringer came along and said, "I feel for you down there."

An objective long-winger saw him and remarked, "It's logical that someone would fall down there."

A car-hawker barely dodged the hole, then yelled out the window, "Now, *that's* a pit!"

A falconer with a hybrid said, "You should've used telemetry."

A Harris hawker came by and said, "If you'd been gang hawking, the others would've helped you."

A gyr flyer said, "If you had listened to me you wouldn't be in that pit."

A dirt-hawker told him to appreciate the terra firma of the pit.

A peregrine falconer said, "It's not about the pit; it's all about the fall."

A raptor biologist saw him and calculated the survival percentage rate for his first year in the pit.

A red-tail hawker missed seeing the man altogether as he scanned the tree tops for squirrels.

An eagle hawker gave him a lecture on "The Elementary Principles of the Pit."

A raptor breeder/geneticist said, "You will die in the pit so you can't produce any more pit-falling offspring."

A kestrel falconer asked, "What's your telemetry frequency?"

A self-pitying Cooper's hawker said, "You haven't seen anything until you've seen my pit!"

An optimistic merlin falconer said, "Things could get worse."

A pessimistic goshawker said, "Things will get worse."

But a dicky-birder saw the man in the pit, took him by the hand and lifted him out.

Adapted from "The Parable of the Pit" by Kenn Filkins — see Page 175.

My hoods; some I made, others — the good ones — I purchased.

Chapter 19
Hoodwinking

Every time I need a hood, it's an emergency.

Usually I spend six weeks getting a hood only to have my female downy grow into a tiercel. Or, after obtaining a beautiful, colorful hood that's a "perfect fit," I go hawking and I lose it.

The emergency is then compounded by the need to convince the *Chairman* of its urgency. Sometimes I think it's no divine accident that the start of the hawking season coincides with the opening of school. The Chairman's concerns are more for school clothes and hot lunches than for necessities like — well — like a hood.

When the formal request comes before the finance committee we discuss the necessity of falconry equipment along with refinishing the hardwood floors, then I bring up the abundance of shoes and books. I have never mentioned this to the Chairman, but have you ever considered the similarity between the words mascara and masquerade? The Chairman often alludes to the number of hoods on hand. The total is 35 in my office, not including the one hanging on my hawking bag, the two above the stove, the one in the van or those in the bedroom. Some of the hoods, I will freely admit, are totally worthless, yet they are kept for their sentimental value. These were not counted.

Thirty-five is not really many, just consider this: There are several styles of hoods including Dutch, Arab, Afghan, Indian, Rufter, Anglo/Indian and even a few that defy classification! Now each style has its own set of advantages and problems; therefore one cannot just use any style on any raptor. Some of the 35 are special patterns designed for certain species.

Secondly, hoods come in an almost endless number of sizes, at least one for each sex of every species. And every species has its unusually large and small individuals, who require a different size. For Harris hawks, I have six hood sizes: one each for small hens, small males, average hens, average males, large hens, and large males. Hybrid falcons have created a whole new category for the hoodmaker. Individuals from the same hybrid cross can vary greatly in head shape.

I even have some sizes that don't fit any particular bird or species. But falconers know from experience that we always end up with that one unique bird for which we have no hood. I will confess, even if only in private, that I do have two of some sizes, but they are different colors! And I never know when I may have two birds of the same sex and species and with my luck I will need to hood them at the same time. Besides, there is an unwritten law that says no hood is ever "a perfect fit" on more than one hawk. Have you ever tried to wear someone else's leather shoes?

This count did not include the hoods I have lost over the years, or the ones I have thrown out — a cardinal sin, I confess — or the ones that have been destroyed or eaten by the dog.

The Chairman used to ask, "Why don't you make your own hoods?"

Lord knows, I have all the stuff to make one. My supplies include kip, kangaroo hides, three complete sets of different patterns, dye in 10-15 colors (some "custom" mixed), brushes, blocks, two sets of leather tools, forceps, three awls, waxed and unwaxed thread, two stitch markers, needles, *special* scissors, three leather punches, four kinds of glue, five types of surgical knives, feathers for plumes, leather stamps... In my earlier years I knew the answer to my poor hood making was "new leather tools."

Just take my first hood for example. It was for a passage red-tailed hawk. I had no patterns, but I could see a couple of male red-tails in a local zoo from a distance of 10 yards. I knew I could do it. After all, I had just passed my falconry exam. In retrospect that alone was a major miracle, as I had only "old" texts on falconry to study. They talked about seeling, raggle and useful things of that sort (hint: they are not on the test).

My first hood was a Dutch style with beautiful gold leather (suede actually) and blue satin on the eye patches. It was carefully stitched (with monofilament). I didn't have any blocks so I designed a method to make the eye patches bulge out. I would be glad to share it with one and all, for a SASE.

After hours and days of diligent work, I took it to the only falconer I knew. He smiled, put his fist inside and said that it just might be

PHOTO COURTESY OF KEN HOOKE

The "Wodan" Khan hood made by a hood maker, artist and falconer, Ken Hooke, of Winnipeg, Manitoba. To see more of Hooke's colorful hoods go to his website at www.falconryhoodsinternational.com or email him at ken@falconryhoodsinternational.com.

small enough to fit a very large female golden eagle. "Well," I thought, "I might get a golden eagle someday!" He traced some Anglo/Indian patterns for me. The smaller patterns and lighter, thinner leather were much harder to work with. And the turkish knot! The only tight knots I got were in my stomach. Braces. . . well, the best pair I ever had were in my mouth. What the Chairman clearly does not understand, is how this futile effort causes me to freely pay so much for so little brightly colored leather.

Before I ask for my 36th hood, I'll take a look at the shoe racks and several large boxes of books. Then it may not be as hard to hoodwink the Chairman as one might suppose.

Joe Ballone's once-intermewed passage red-tailed hawk, Mystic, pursues a gray squirrel that darted to the far side of a hardwood tree in a cemetery.

Chapter 20 ~~Fine Weather For Ducks~~ *squirrels*

Several mallards rested quietly on a small calm creek. Their tranquil afternoon was about to be disturbed.

Unseen by the ducks, Joe Ballone and I silently slipped closer to the creek with Harris hawks on our gloves. As we popped over the bank, the ducks scrambled into flight as Sadie and Samwise launched their attack. Sam, a male baywing, missed his selected target. But Sadie, a female Harris, grabbed a drake as it lifted off the water. When she hit it the mallard plunged back into the chilly water. Sadie hung on. She looked back over her shoulder as the submerged duck towed her toward the opposite bank.

I was indecisive on what to do next. Should I jump in and grab both of them?

Along Lake Superior

As I drove that morning, across the Upper Peninsula, from Sault Ste. Marie to Marquette, the weather seemed indecisive, too. On the three-hour ride along the shore of Lake Superior, every 15 miles the road conditions varied from sunny and snow-free to dark clouds and heavy snowfall, to bright sun on a snowy forest of green cedars, back to a blast of snow driven by hard winds off the world's largest freshwater lake. As the hours past, I wondered what weather would greet us in Marquette. To me it looked like fine weather for ducks. We had moved back the start time for the inaugural Upper Peninsula Hawking Meet. We knew we would have 100 percent participation — two falconers — on Black Friday, the shopping day after Thanksgiving, 2009. Our plan was to fly Mystic, Joe's intermewed red-tailed hawk at squirrels and my three Harris hawks at ducks. The weather in Marquette was calm and cool with a skiff of snow on the ground.

How Deep?

"How deep is the creek?" I asked Joe as Sadie floated with her wings and tail spread widely.

"Not all that deep," he said as I wondered if I should take my cell phone out of my pocket.

Then the duck tried to pull Sadie under the water. She went so far down that only her wing tips and head were out of the cold water.

I jumped in. She popped back up. As I sloshed toward her with all the subtlety of a bull moose, the duck somehow got free, popped up and flew off.

Soaked from the waist down, I scooped her up and walked back to the bank.

"My indecision cost her a duck," I lamented to Joe. "I should have decided beforehand to dive in if it took her into the creek."

"Well, let's go to the next bend," Joe suggested, "where we saw the other ducks."

At that spot, both Sam and Sadie grabbed drakes, which immediately dragged them into the icy water. Before I could jump in, the ducks were free and the Harris hawks began their "swim" to the opposite bank. After retrieving the soaked baywings, I changed into dry clothes in the public restroom of a nearby hockey rink.

Earlier that morning my wife Marti asked me why I was taking extra clothes on the trip.

"Are you spending the night?" she asked.

"No. We're duck hawking," I replied. "I may get wet."

I didn't remind her of the jackrabbit rescue incident.

To give the hawks time to dry off, we turned out attention to squirrels.

"Guard That Tree"

At one of Joe's squirrel hotspots, he spotted a gray squirrel scampering near the base of a hardwood tree.

"You guard that tree," Joe instructed, as he pointed at a nearby mature tree. "They often try to get into that tree and escape in that slit in the trunk."

Toting my camera, I placed myself between the squirrel tree and the "slit tree," as Mystic took a high perch. She began searching the branches for her quarry. It soon became obvious it was not her first rodeo. Once the squirrel was spotted, Mystic seemed to plan her

Mystic chases a gray squirrel in a tree in Marquette, Michigan.

attack. She watched for an opportunity, then bolted from a neighboring tree and tried to scrape the squirrel off a branch or trunk. She pressured the squirrel so hard in the first couple flights that the squirrel panicked. It made a fateful hesitation, then scrambled down the trunk and leaped to the ground. As it ran around me, I realized that in all the excitement, I had failed. It was my indecision again: photograph the flight or participate in it. The squirrel bounded quickly toward the escape tree. With safety only a couple feet away, a brown blur blazed in from the left and a huge yellow foot reached out and snatched the gray squirrel in mid-jump. Mystic's wingtip marks in the skit of snow were evidence of her decisiveness.

"That was awesome," I told Joe. "Now what do we do? The Harris are still soaked."

"Well, she has never taken two squirrels in one day," Joe said, then added, "That was the first squirrel she's taken on the ground."

"Let's give her another try," I suggested. "This looks like good weather for squirrels."

As we approached a more tightly-wooded location, Joe saw two squirrels on the ground near a stand of pine trees. The squirrels sought shelter in the pines as Mystic took an initial perch about 50 feet away. She laddered up this tree and then did a long, fast flight and tried to scrape the squirrel off the tree trunk. She didn't connect, but made a loud thump as she flew into and through the tree. After missing, she took a perch on the end of a pine bow in a nearby tree. She sat there for about three minutes, then charged and grabbed the squirrel which was moving from tree to tree. Mystic snagged the gray squirrel from the branch and they tumbled downward. They hit a dead limb as they fell, it broke off and struck Joe on his head as he ran over to assist Mystic. This was her first double with squirrels and Joe was pumped. Mystic stepped off the kill for a couple tidbits and we had our second squirrel in the bag in less than 15 minutes.

"Well, as easy as she came off that one, we should find her a third one," I said. "Mystic needs to get her Hat Trick."

"Whatever you want," Joe said. "I'm happy with two."

Mystic battles with one of the squirrels caught on Black Friday.

Just Ducky

"Let's see what we can find," I urged. "If we find a duck slip on the way to the next spot, we'll give the Harris hawks a try."

We searched for squirrels and found some but too many folks were afoot walking their dogs — some in areas that prohibit dogs — that we did not get a slip.

So we intensified our search for waterfowl in several creeks, small ponds and ditches. We had a few great chases with the still-wet Harris hawks but none resulted in a catch as the mallards quickly turned back into the safety of the water. Finally we located some ducks foraging away from a small pond and slipped Sadie off the glove. She bolted after a drake and tail-chased it so hard that it became indecisive and flew head first into a chain-link fence. It almost knocked itself out. Sadie avoided the fence then grabbed it.

"That was quick," I said with a smile as wide as Lake Superior. "Let's go back to the first squirrel stop and check a couple duck spots along the way."

Tale of the Black Squirrel Tail

At the first woods, I spotted a black squirrel.

"There's a black squirrel," I said pointing off in the distance. "I think it's at the slit-tree."

"She's never taken a black squirrel," Joe said. "But she has only seen one."

"Let's catch that one," I cheered.

As we approached, the black one ran up the slit-tree. Joe released Mystic and posted me at the slit with a brush beating stick. The five foot long slit was seven feet up in the tree, so I could defend the length of it with the stick. Our first encounter with this tree motivated me to defend this escape hole with great vigor. I knew that if this squirrel made it into this hole, Joe would never let me forget it.

"I've been waiting to get a black squirrel," Joe said later. "And it was as if the stars had aligned."

He put Mystic up, and it seemed like the squirrel was making all the wrong moves. It climbed to the top of the hardwood tree, then it ran out on an upper limb. It appeared to think about jumping to another tree, but it was indecisive and just sat there. It was wide open for an arial attack. The only problem was Mystic seemed indifferent and indecisive about this squirrel.

She then chased it but not hard. At one point the squirrel ran down the trunk within a couple feet of her and she just watched it. It then came down to the slit. I yelled and waved the stick and the squirrel scampered down to the ground. It then ran under my van and up a small pine tree. Mystic bolted over and grabbed the squirrel's tail with both feet. As the squirrel struggled to slip free, Mystic kept switching feet on the tail, like a sailor pulling a rope hand-over-hand. But the squirrel finally pulled its tail free. It scrambled down and across a yard then underneath a bench which was built around the base of a tree. Mystic charged under the bench and slammed into to garden fencing the squirrel slipped through. The last we saw was the black squirrel tail disappearing into the hole of a tree.

Fading Light

After hawking all afternoon, the light began fading on both Mystic's attempt at her first squirrel hat-trick and more duck slips for the Harris hawks.

We returned to recheck a favorite squirrel spot that was also near a possible duck pond. As the darkness settled, a quietness blanketed the woods. As we pulled through, Joe was not feeling too confident about finding another squirrel. I reminded him that squirrels are cre-puscular — most active at dawn and dusk — though I too was doubt-ful that we'd see any more climbing critters. A few seconds later I spotted a squirrel in a small tree. Joe got Mystic out. She flew strong and right away had the gray squirrel on the move. It looked to be try-ing to get deeper in the woods and had jumped to another tree as Mystic charged in to scrape it off the branch. She missed and pitched up to another tree, just as the squirrel scurried down and started run-ning in her direction. Joe ran after the squirrel and was keyed in on her when Mystic flashed in and slammed it into the ground.

I let out a thunderous cheer loud enough to raise the dead.

The silence was broken.

The hat was tossed.

Mystic had three squirrels.

Our day was done.

Or, So We Thought

As we left the woods, we had enough light to check out the nearby duck spot. We found some mallards feeding in the grass near a tiny pond. We ambushed the small flock and Sam chased a drake back toward the pond. He grabbed it as they got to the edge of the pond and both went into the frigid water. Joe was the closest one to him, so — without any delay or indecision — he jumped into the calf-deep water. He reached under Sam to grab the duck, but when he pulled up he only had a hold of the hawk. Not wanting to pull Sam off the duck,

Ballone pauses with Mystic and her "Hat-Trick" of gray squirrels.

Joe let go. The birds fell back into the pond and the duck began to pull Sam deeper. Joe followed, now thigh-deep. Each time its head surfaced, Joe grabbed at the duck, it would dive and swim deeper. Soon, Joe was hip-deep. Again, it was rinse-and-repeat. By the time Joe got his hands on the wayward mallard, he was chest-deep in the pond.

But through Joe's selfless efforts, Sam had his first duck.

This ended the inaugural "Upper Peninsula Hawking Meet." There will be "Second Annual Upper Peninsula Hawking Meet."

About that we're not indecisive.

On Wings Like Eagles

Chapter 21
On Wings Like Eagles
Isaiah 40:31

Who has not marveled at the effortless soaring of a bird overhead? Eagles are the largest and most majestic of all as they stretch their wings and soar aloft. The prophets Isaiah and Moses both use the eagle's effortless flight to illustrate the strength God gives to believers. Moses wrote that Israel was brought out of Egypt "on eagle's wings." (Exodus 19:4)

As a falconer and preacher, I have always drawn to Isaiah's eagle passage:

> Yet those who wait for the Lord
> Will gain new strength;
> They will mount up on wings like eagles.
> They will run and not get tired.
> They will walk and not become weary.
> (Isaiah 40:31 — NASB)

A misconception of this passage revolves around this popular illustration. A mother eagle using food tempts her young eaglet out of the nest on his first flight. As the young bird tries his wings, he falters and tumbles earthward. The mother, seeing the distress of her offspring, swoops down under him in a breathtaking dive catching him on her back. The eaglet is then "mounted up on the wings of an eagle." He is returned to the security of the nest until she leads him on yet another adventure in faith.

An eaglet old enough to fly is as large as an adult eagle and is clumsy, like a teenager whose body has developed faster than his coordination. Because eagles can carry only one-half their weight, it is an aerodynamic and physical impossibility for the mother eagle to carry him. A Chinese proverbs also tells the impossibility of the scenario. "If you tie two birds together, although they have four wings they still cannot fly."

What then is Isaiah's point if the eagle cannot perform this lovely but unrealistic feat?

Strength provided

Isaiah provides a picture of God's strength for the weary through the eagle's effortless soaring. Eagles do not soar on their own power and strength alone. They are heavy birds and spend a great deal of flying time searching for food. If the eagles had to exert the energy to sustain their weight in flight for that long a time, they may grow weak. That weariness could result in an inability to capture quarry which could result in a slow miserable death by starvation.

This can be equated with the despair one feels when trying to earn salvation by his own merit or works: "For the wages of sin is death," (Romans 6:23).

Therefore, God provides the eagles with strength outside their own ability. God provids hot air thermals. Eagles can ride these thermals tirelessly for hours in search of quarry. God provides us with grace and forgiveness — that we need so desperately but did not deserve — nor could we obtain it on own merit. "But the free gift of God is eternal life in Christ Jesus our Lord," (Romans 6:23).

The sun shining upon the earth's irregular surface heats the air above the ground unevenly, thereby causing great volumes of air to rise above their neighbors. They ascend as invisible enormous bubbles in the manner of a hot-air balloon. They are called thermal currents — streams of rising hot air. Eagles and other raptors circle on the lift created on the outer ridge of such currents.

Soaring Eagles

A raptor flying on motionless outstretched wings is for all intents and purposes a glider. The wings and tail control the downward movement by transforming it into a forward thrust, which nevertheless moves on a declining line. The rate of descent which is in terms of "sinking speed," is given in feet-per-second (ft/sec).

Let us assume the sinking speed of an eagle is 3 ft/sec. That means that during every second of his flight in still air he loses three feet in height. However, when he enters one of the invisible "balloons," air mass raises at a rate of 10 ft/sec. Therefore the eagle's relative movement to the ground is 10 - 3 = 7 ft/sec upward! While the eagle

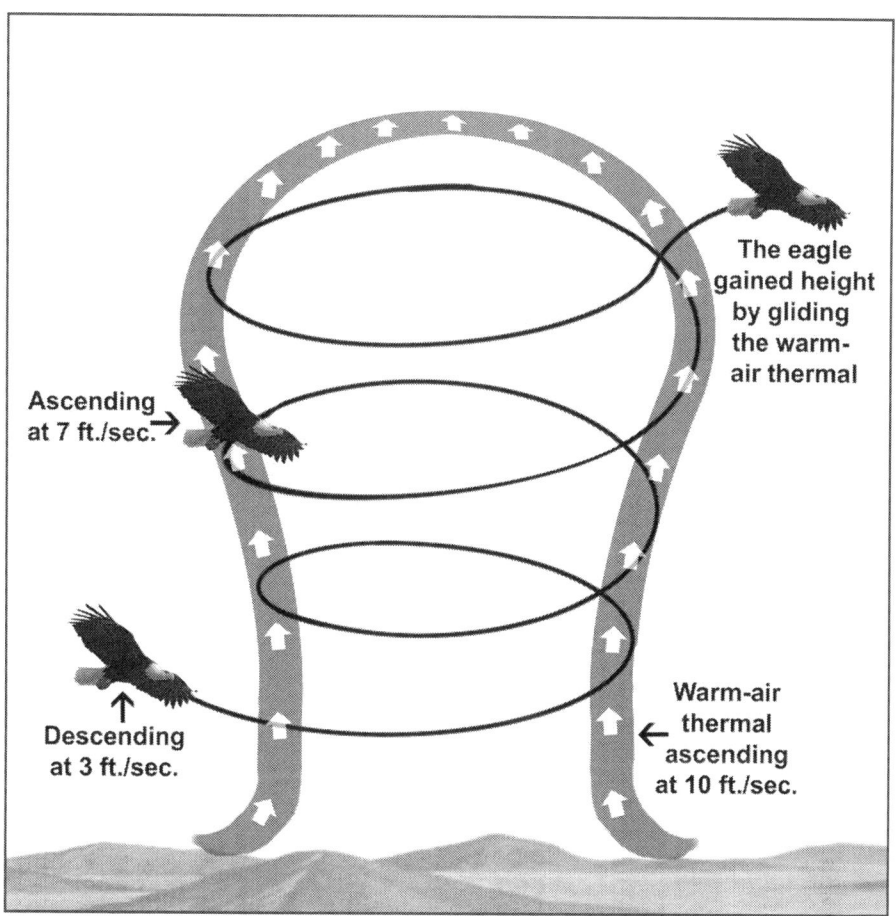

Suppose the sinking speed of a gliding eagle is 3 ft/sec and the invisible warm-air thermal raises at a rate of 10 ft/sec. Therefore the eagle's relative movement to the ground is 10 - 3 = 7 ft/sec upward! While the eagle descends in relationship to the surrounding air, he still gains height in relationship to the ground.

descends in relationship to the surrounding air, he still gains height in relationship to the ground. The hot-air bubble climbs faster than the eagle falls. So while the bird loses height within the balloon, he still goes up with it.

If we allow the thermal current to illustrate God's grace and forgiveness, then the eagle's descent within it illustrates how we are in God's grace, yet "fall short of the glory of God," (Romans 3:23). The eagle's ascent in relationship to the ground illustrates that the Christian is maturing while becoming separate from the desires of the world.

Pride comes when a Christian evaluates himself in relationship to the ground. "Look how high I am! I'm better than the world and its people." Humility comes when he evaluates himself in relationship to the thermal of grace — "I may be maturing but I need to be more like Jesus."

Pride comes when we evaluate ourselves with other sinners. Humility comes when we compare ourselves with Christ.

Relying on God

The eagle must rely daily upon God's strength to sustain life, yet by God's provisions the eagle not only survives but excels as one of His most majestic creations. Christians can excel by "flying by faith." This divinely-sustained flight is dependent upon our relationship with God.

"Yet those who wait for the Lord will gain new strength." This "waiting" is like the service of a waiter or waitress. The Old Testament reveals the character of one who "waits for the Lord" not one who waits idly by, rather as an active follower with a heart open to God's leading.

One who waits for the Lord will:
* have a repentant and teachable heart (Psalm 25:3-5),
* have a desire for integrity and righteousness (Psalm 25:21),
* have a heart of prayer (Psalm 40:1),
* have a trust in God's word and faithfulness (Psalm 130:5),
* not repay evil for evil (Proverbs 20:22).

Just as the eagles soar in obedience to God's natural laws, so we have success by observing God's natural and spiritual laws. The one who waits upon the Lord obeys God's principles for living. Psalm 37:34 teaches that those waiting for the Lord will "keep His way."

Soaring Christians

A person with this kind of character will receive God's strength. Like eagles, we must exercise our faith in God's word and principles. As an eagle without flight is dead, so "faith without works is dead" (James 2:26). The eagle that can fly yet does not express that belief by leaving his nest of security will soon die of starvation. So will the Christian who is unwilling to leave his worldly security and live by faith.

The rich young ruler was a "grounded eagle," unable to leave the security of his wealth to soar on God's strength. For the most part the Jewish leaders were unwilling to leave the security of their religious and social position to glide on God's grace. Paul was one of many who cast off all other securities and counted them as loss to know the surpassing greatness of Christ and His strength. "I can do all things through Him who strengthens me" (Philippians 4:13).

In our society filled with fitness centers, aerobic classes and elliptical machines, Isaiah's statement is still true. Youths grow weary and tired and vigorous young men stumble badly, yet those who wait upon the Lord will gain new strength: They will mount up with wings like eagles.

A pair of bald eagles rest in the trees along Lake Superior near Brimley, Michigan.

PHOTO BY MARTI FILKINS

Sadie and Samwise flew in a cast since they were 12 weeks old. Rarely did they hunt without each other or with other Harris hawks.

Chapter 22
Five for One

For decades, I avoided squirrel hunting with Harris hawks.

But living in Sault Ste. *Siberia* forced me to change my hawking paradigm.

The snowshoe hare — our only local rabbits — have been in a long low-cycle that some blame on the recently released and highly successful wolves. Longtime local hare hunters reported the nearly complete absence of snowshoes. Cottontails are three hours south of the Sault on I-75.

The cast has caught crows, ducks, pigeons, starlings, cottontails, jackrabbits and other critters but rarely squirrels.

I've avoided pursuing these thick-skinned biting beasts because they're dangerous critters. A squirrel bite can sever a tendon and permanently disable a hunting hawk — especially Harris hawks with their strong but slender toes.

Sure the flights were exciting, with the three-dimensional action and aerial assaults as a squirrel tries to bridge from the top of one tree to another. But the danger was never worth the thrill when non-biting rabbits were available.

Here, there are no cottontails.

I frequently drive three to four hours to hawk bunnies, but weekend hawking is never enough.

Paradigm Shift

In recent years I've grudgingly shifted my hawking paradigm.

Now Sadie, Samwise and Gabi — my trio of Harris hawks — hunt squirrels with intent to do bodily harm.

Each day's hawking gear now includes a medical kit and an ice pick to quickly vanquish the bushy-tailed demons.

In early December, more than a foot of snow fell on Sault Ste. Marie, which made seed piles in the woods more alluring to the tree climbers. At an abandoned campground near the local university, no squirrels were spotted from the road. The cast was released on speculation, and squirrel tracks were found coming and going from a black thistle seed pile at the base of a dead tree.

As we neared that tree Sadie flew intently toward the tree where Joe's red-tail Ember caught her first black squirrel. As Sadie laddered up the tree I knew she had spotted our quarry.

Since we had hunted this section of woods before I knew where we had lost three squirrels that took refuge in nearby holes. Two climbers had escaped in a small tree's belt-buckle-high hole and a third disappeared in a large tree with a chest-high hole. Guarding them was a key element to success, and both trees were marked with yellow caution tape.

Fine Whine

As I scanned for the location of the tape and the holes, Sadie whined.

When I hear that call, I know something is in mortal danger.

Moments later the squirrel darted down from the top of the tree. Sadie tried to scrape it off the trunk as it descended. The buck barely eluded her and climbed back up when she and Sam were out of position. Then it bridged over to the tree that climbers run down before disappearing into the belt-buckle-high hole. Having been hoodwinked at this spot twice before, I ran to the yellow tape and blocked the bushy-tail's escape.

When the buck saw me he continued through the top of that tree and crossed to the next tree, toward the chest-high hole. It quickly scrambled through three more trees as Sadie and Sam tried to snatch it between the tree tops. I took my eyes off the quarry and raptors and ran as fast as I could in the deep snow, downed logs and branches to that second escape hole. I was three feet away when the squirrel darted around the tree toward the hole.

I could almost see the surprise on its face. I expected it would continue into the hole, as I was not quick enough to stop it. But to my astonishment the startled buck instantly turned back and climbed back up the tree.

It traced its path back toward the pursuing hawks. I ran back to the belt-buckle-high hole. As the climber crossed on the final bridge, Sadie grabbed it. They became hung up on a secondary branch and battled as Sadie tried to get a grip on its business end. Somehow they fell and the squirrel hit the ground before Sadie. From three feet away I saw Sadie strike with her left foot as the buck opened its mouth to bite her. She shoved her foot right into its mouth. Panicking at that sight, I dropped to the ground to help her. But she released the beast and it darted up the tree. It was only five feet from the belt-buckle-high hole, but I blocked the path.

Bridging Back

It kept climbing, bridged back to the original tree, then through two more trees before stopping in a tree near a vehicle path. The wide lane created space between the branches of the trees on opposite sides.

There was no bridge.

The tree had no holes. Sam took a high perch nearby and the squirrel froze. It had blood on it's face. Was it the squirrel's or Sadie's? I wondered, or both? Sadie bled profusely but, thankfully, no permanent damage occurred from the bite.

Sadie flew to a low branch in a small tree.

To some it may appear that she was pouting or sulking.

She was not.

Adrenaline Rush

She had such a rush of adrenaline while chasing squirrel that she needed time to rebound from the adrenaline crash.

Sadie clearly showed that a week before at the woods near a gravel pit. We hunted the familiar site on speculation. She led the hunt that day. She would spot a squirrel, drive it out of the tree and crash through the brush to get to it. Sam followed her lead and both had close strikes. Sadie did this six or seven times — it may have included a reflush of a squirrel or two. She was on fire during every chase. Finally, she led the charge after a gray at the edge of the woods. By the time I got through the thick cover to the hawks, the climber was out of sight.

As we left the area Sadie flew back and attacked the squirrel as it scrambled down a 45-degree tree trunk. The tree's roots were sticking up in the air creating a barrier with the brush and saplings that had grown after the tree fell. Sadie flew down the slanted tree and almost connected as the creature ran inside the barrier. It made a mistake as it tried to escape by running to a larger tree a few feet away.

Sadie pitched up off the roots then rolled into a pumping stoop and hit the beast less then 18 inches from the brush. Moments later when

I got to Sadie, as she was mantling, her whole body was shaking from the adrenaline rush. She may have the same explosion of adrenaline when she sees a jackrabbit, but on the long flights she may burn that off during the flight.

A Fifth Time

While Sadie recovered from her crash, Samwise kept the squirrel from moving. A few minutes later, Sadie perked up and began laddering up the escape tree. Soon after that, Sadie was chasing that squirrel with the same passion as before. She took three different shots at it and almost scraped it off the tree. Sadie pitch over to a nearby tree. As the quarry darted down the trunk Sam bolted after it and snatched the beast off the tree.

Spinning like a wounded helicopter, they fell toward the deep snow. As they crashed into the snow, the squirrel got free for the third time. It made two bounds and Sadie slammed into it as it passed under a downed tree. Sadie was knocked off — its forth escape.

I bolted to the belt-buckle hole as the squirrel raced through the tree tops to beat me there.

Sadie was instantly back in pursuit as the squirrel and I met at the small tree again. It bridged toward the large tree hole again, but Sadie grabbed the buck in the same branches as their first encounter. She snatched him from the branches and made a more controlled decent that Sam did. They hit the deep snow hard enough that Sadie was up to her chest in snow. I dropped to my knees and reached through the snow from both sides to grab the squirrel.

When I pulled it up, Sadie had both feet planted on its head.

After the fifth time. . .

The beast was dead.

Samwise mantles over a gray squirrel he snatched off the trunk of a tree in our back yard.

A red-tailed hawk raises her feet to gently land on Mike Evan's glove. When chasing quarry, red-tails crash into brush like a sledgehammer. This red-tail has squirrel chaps — made by Evans, of Sturgis, Michigan — on her ankles to protect her from squirrel bites.

Chapter 23
Ted's Tender Tush

One fine fall day, Ted Nusbaum flew his male Harris hawk, Shogun, while Dale Barnett flew his passage red-tailed hawk in the same field. Their unusual arrangement worked well. Though the two hawks did not fly as a cast, they tolerated each other in the field.

All was fine until Shogun snagged a cottontail in a field near Rolling Prairie.

The rabbit squealed as Ted ran toward them.

Dale yelled as his passage hawk bolted out of a tree.

"Watch out," he screamed, "here comes my hawk!"

Dale's red-tail pumped hard and fast intent on claiming a share of the bunny.

He tried to call the hawk down, but she was intently focused on the Harris hawk and the quarry.

We feared she would crash into Shogun before Ted could intervene.

Ted won the race.

With his back to the excited red-tail, Ted knelt next to his hawk and leaned over the top of bird and rabbit. Ted sheltered Shogun with his legs, body and arms from the attacking hawk.

Apparently the passage bird could still see a glimpse of the Harris between Ted's thighs.

With the force of a red-tail crashing heavy brush, the hawk slammed feet first into Ted's tush.

Ted screamed.

We panicked thinking Dale's hawk had Shogun by the head.

"Where did she grab your hawk?" I asked as we ran up, "By the head?"

"She doesn't have my hawk," Ted said excitedly, "She has *me!*"

"What?" Dale asked.

"Her talon is in my butt crack," Ted divulged.

The hawk's talons had penetrated Ted's jeans and underwear within reach of a tender area between his cheeks.

When we realized the hawk was fine, Dale and I started chuckling, as the excited red-tail hung from Ted's derriere.

"When I move, the grips tighter," Ted explained. "And her talon goes up my crack."

Obviously, it was a tender situation.

Then Dale mimicked the squeak of a mouse.

The red-tail squeezed Ted's crack all the harder.

He moaned.

We laughed.

"Hey, this hurts," Ted cried out.

Dale squeaked again.

Ted cursed.

We roared all the louder.

"Dale, stop that," Ted said sternly. "And get her off me. . . carefully."

After a few more minutes to compose ourselves, Dale tempted her off of Ted's heinie with a tidbit.

Ted's tender tush incurred no longterm injury. . .

That he would admit to anyway.

Co-inventing Car-hawking

When he was not covering his bottom, Ted and fellow falconer Bill Boler co-invented car-hawking in northern Indiana.

In 1982 Ted and Bill introduced me to car-hawking which was later reported in the 1984 *NAFA Journal.* From that small beginning car-hawking has spread across North America and the world. A quick check on YouTube proves it.

Bill and Ted's excellent adventure in car-hawking began with flying kestrel falcons out the window at starlings. Ted told of a time he slipped his tiny kestrel at a large pigeon. The bold kestrel bound to the pigeon which simply flew off, "as easily as a grizzly bear could run with a man on its back," Ted said.

Next they looked for ways to catch crows with a hawk, so they started flying red-tailed hawks out from a van. The next generation of car-hawking began when they flew Harris hawks. One August, they traveled to the Indiana Falconers' Association's Summer Picnic at La

Mans Academy, organized by a falconer and my friend Brother Ed Mattingly of Rolling Prairie. On their 32-mile journey they caught a gaggle of starlings with a Harris hawk. Most falconers were in disbelief.

I had no doubt.

Previously, we had hawked out of Ted's blue Ford Econoline van. Ted and I sat in the back while holding our Harris hawks on the glove with the side-door wide open. When quarry presented itself, the chase was on. It was great fun.

And history was made.

Sarah and Shogun II hang out in the weathering area in Rolling Prairie, Indiana.

A passage red-tailed hawk returns to Scott Stratton's glove at a Michigan Hawking Club Meet. The fact that falconry birds are released to fly free shows that hawks and falcons stay with the falconer because they choose to remain. Falconry is neither pet-keeping nor like a zoo; the raptors are free to leave or stay.

Chapter 24
Animal Rights — Christian Morals

Years ago, a national Christian magazine published my article titled "Animal Rights — Christian Morals."

A church member for Illinois sent a threatening letter to the magazine's editor. She wrote, "I don't know who Kenn Filkins is or what kind of editor you think you are, but if you ever print an article like that again I will quit reading your magazine and withdraw my membership from the church."

The editor wrote me an encouraging note saying, "I guess this lady doesn't think too much of either one of us."

Decades later, the debate about animal rights rages on.

As a Christian and a minister of the Gospel, I've been asked about the assumed conflict between hunting animals — with or without a raptor — with my Christian conscience.

One man asked it this way, "How can a preacher of peace be a man of war (against animals)?"

Animal Right or Animal Welfare?

Obviously, no genuine Christian would ever support the neglect, abuse, torture or misuse of animals. Christians — like all people — have a duty to treat animals humanely and with proper care. But that's correctly termed animal welfare, not animal rights.

President Lincoln — who believed in Jesus— said, "I care not much for a man's religion whose dog and cat are not better for it."

Paul Harvey, also a Christian, added this humorous thought: "Ever occur to you why some of us can be this much concerned with animals suffering? Because government is not. Why not? Animals don't vote."

To support their cause, animal rights proponents use this Mark Twain quote, "The fact that man knows right from wrong proves his intellectual superiority to the other creatures; but the fact that he can do wrong proves his moral inferiority to any creatures that cannot," (What is Man, 1906)

Obviously, here Twain commented on the sad condition of fallen man and did not imply that animals have the same rights as humans.

Three Key Issues

As a Christian, the debate revolves around three key questions:
• Are humans just another animal species?
• How does God treat animals?
• Why did the Creator make both predator and prey?

Are humans just another species of animal?

The founding principle of the animal rights movement conflict with Biblical principles.

In 1989, Ingrid Newkirk, the head of the People for the Ethical Treatment of Animals (PETA), stated the matter very succinctly: "Animal Liberationists do not separate out the human animal, so there is no rational basis for saying that a human being has special rights. A rat is a pig is a dog is a boy. They are all mammals."

PETA views "rights" only on the ability to feel pain and suffering. The Christian worldview bases "rights" on the fact that humans were created differently from animals. The Bible draws a clear line between humans and animals. First, humans were created "in the image of God" (Genesis 1:27, 2:7). This means humans have intellect, emotion, will and conscience. Humans also have an everlasting spirit. James affirms that man was created in God's image (James 3:9).

Every human, no matter of what race, intelligence, handicap or level of development, has rights — rights that are distinct from animals over which God granted humans "dominion" (Genesis 1:28-30). The Scriptures clearly place animals under man's stewardship of the earth.

PETA's "human animals" lower mankind to the level of animals. They give animals equal rights by lowering humans to the level of animals.

In his book, *A Rat is a Pig is a Dog is a Boy: The Human Cost of the Animal Rights Movement*, Wesley J. Smith said, "Animal welfare acknowledges that humans have unique dignity and value. In direct contrast, animal rights denigrates human exceptionalism as 'speciesist,' that is, discrimination against animals."

How does God treat animals?

"The basis of all animal rights should be the Golden Rule: We should treat them as we would wish them to treat us, were any other species in our dominant position," said Christine Stevens an animal rights supporter.

PETA's agenda not only strives to bar cosmetics firms from testing products on animals, prevent the slaughter of furry beasts for their pelts alone and halt animal cruelty in laboratories. Their agenda includes: ending all medical research that uses animals, closing all pet shops, ending all animal breeding, ending pet-keeping, ending all meat eating, closing all zoos and circuses and preventing hunting and fishing. They also desire a constitutional change which would provide animals with "the right to life, liberty, and the pursuit of happiness."

God cares for animals. He is certainly a birdwatcher. He provides for them, too (Matthew 6:26).

"Are not two sparrows sold for a cent? And yet not one of them will fall to the ground apart from your Father. . . . So do not fear; you are more valuable than many sparrows" (Matthew 10:29, 31).

Here Jesus does not condemn owning or selling sparrows, and He specifically says humans are "more valuable" than animals.

The correct view of animals can be seen by how God deals with animals. God Himself made Adam and Eve's first clothes from animal pelts (Genesis 3:21), which acknowledges that human needs outweigh those of animals. Animal sacrifice started in the Garden of Eden, when God showed Adam and Eve the result of their disobedience. God caused a strong wind to blow wild quail into the Israelite's wilderness camp for food (Numbers 11:31-32). After the birth of Jesus, Joseph and Mary sacrificed a dove as required by Jewish law (Luke 2:24). At the Last Supper, lamb was undoubtedly served. After Christ's resurrection, he cooked fish for his disciples to eat along the shore of Galilee (John 21:10-13). Jesus rode into Jerusalem on the foal of a donkey — a type of instrumental use of animals deemed immoral by animal rights believers. God even created some animals to be "livestock" (domesticated animals) as well as wild animals, (Genesis 2:19-20).

Smith said, "Animal welfare acknowledges that we may benefit from animal husbandry, but that in so doing, we have the important duty to treat animals humanely and never abuse them or cause them gratuitous suffering. Animal rights believers claim that it is immoral to domesticate animals for any purpose, meaning we should not eat meat, wear leather, conduct animal research, and for some, even own dogs. In other words, the ultimate goals of animal welfare and animal rights are in direct conflict: The former seeks to improve our use of animals; the latter, to end it altogether."

Why did the Creator make both predator and prey?

In promoting his book, Smith said, "I have been told by self-described Christians that the sanctity of life ethic includes animals as well as people, and that the practice of true Christianity requires vegetarianism."

Which of course makes no sense from a Christian worldview, especially in light of predation in nature. If, as the animal rights believers say, killing an animal is not different than murdering a person, than a lioness that kills a wildebeest to feed her cub, is a murderer. Should the lioness be put to death as a murderer, according to animal rights principles?

The animal rights members would rebut, "No, she should not be harmed because she is only doing what is natural for her."

My point exactly.

It's natural.

It's nature's way.

Wildlife biologists have long acknowledged that predation actually benefits the prey species.

Predation is natural.

But animal rights believers think it's unnatural for humans to hunt.

"Regardless of the approach, to the animal rights true believer," Smith said, "what is done to an animal should be judged as if the same action were done to a human being. Hence, animal rightists believe cattle ranching to be as odious as slavery and research on lab rats an equivalent evil to Mengele's experiments in the (Nazi death) camps."

If such were the case, God would never condone hunting. But the Lord did condone it and even honored a "mighty hunter before the Lord."

"Now Cush became the father of Nimrod; he became a mighty one on the earth. He was a mighty hunter before the LORD; therefore it is said, 'Like Nimrod a mighty hunter before the Lord'" (Genesis 10:8, 9, NASB).

Our culture uses the term "Nimrod" as an insult but in the Bible it's a name of honor. Nimrod used his hunting ability to honor the God.

To animal rights groups the verse would mean, "A mighty murderer

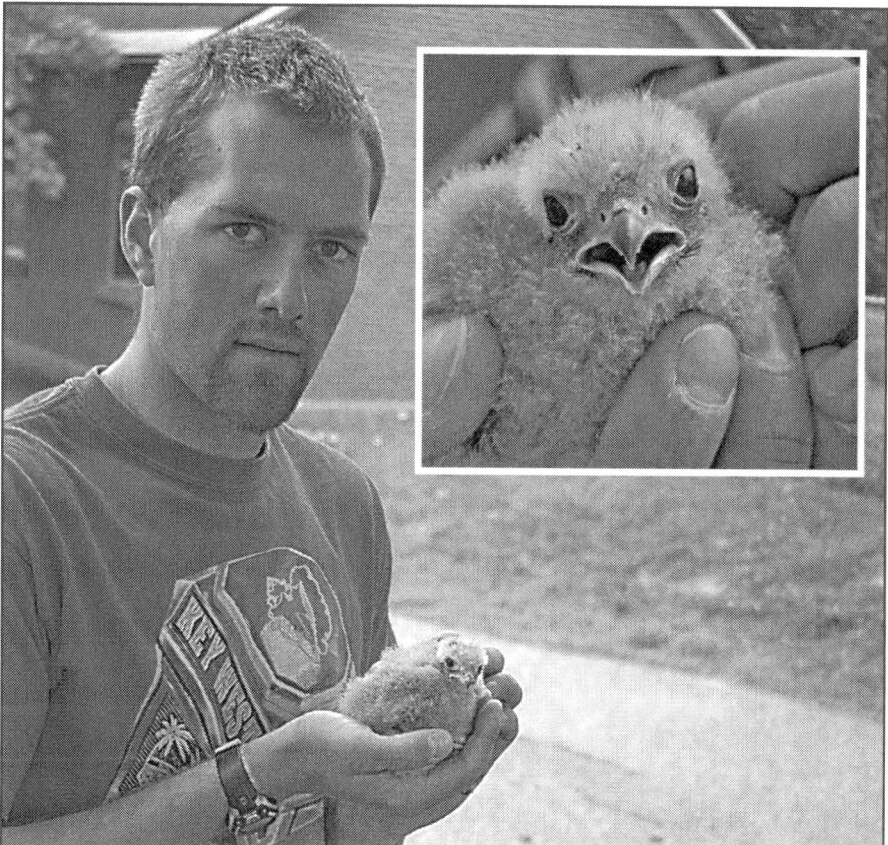

Falconers are actively involved in saving raptors, like this merlin falcon chick. Lake Superior State University Chris Pollard picked the young chick off the campus lawn then contacted a local falconer for help.

before the Lord." God said in the Ten Commandments, "You shall not murder." How could someone who is a murderer be honored by God. Obviously hunting does not oppose the will of God, He honored a man for his skill.

Animals are not human and therefore are not protected under the commandment, "Thou shall not kill" (Exodus 20:13).

Falconry: The Purest Form of Hunting

Of all field sports, falconry is the purist form of hunting. It's "natural" hunting. The hawks, falcons and eagles were born to hunt. Falconry raptors are like professional athletes under the care of a physical trainer or coach. The raptors are hungry, and falconers build up their condition and strength to pursue their quarry.

Falconry is not like a zoo or pet-keeping where raptors are kept in cages. Every time a falconer takes his bird of prey hunting it is released. It is free. It only comes back to the falconer if it chooses to return. It is free to leave and never come back. Still it returns.

There's no denying the fact that falconry birds have a choice to stay or leave.

There is nothing morally or ethically wrong with legal hunting and fishing. Animals should be treated in a kind and humane manner not because animals have rights but because they are under our stewardship within God's creation.

Compassion for People

Yet our concern for the animal kingdom should not outweigh that for people in need and those suffering.

Some years ago, millions of dollars and hundreds of man-hours were spent to free the whales trapped in the arctic ice. Saving trapped whales is a worthy cause. But should not similar outpourings of effort, money and compassion be extended to people in daily need? Animal rights activists call for caged animals everywhere to be freed. But what about people who are caged by bars, illness, poverty, addiction or sin?

Jesus said, "I was sick, and you visited me; I was in prison, and you came to me" (see Matthew 25:35-36).

To those who met the needs of humans, Jesus said, "Come, you blessed of My Father, inherit the kingdom prepared for you."

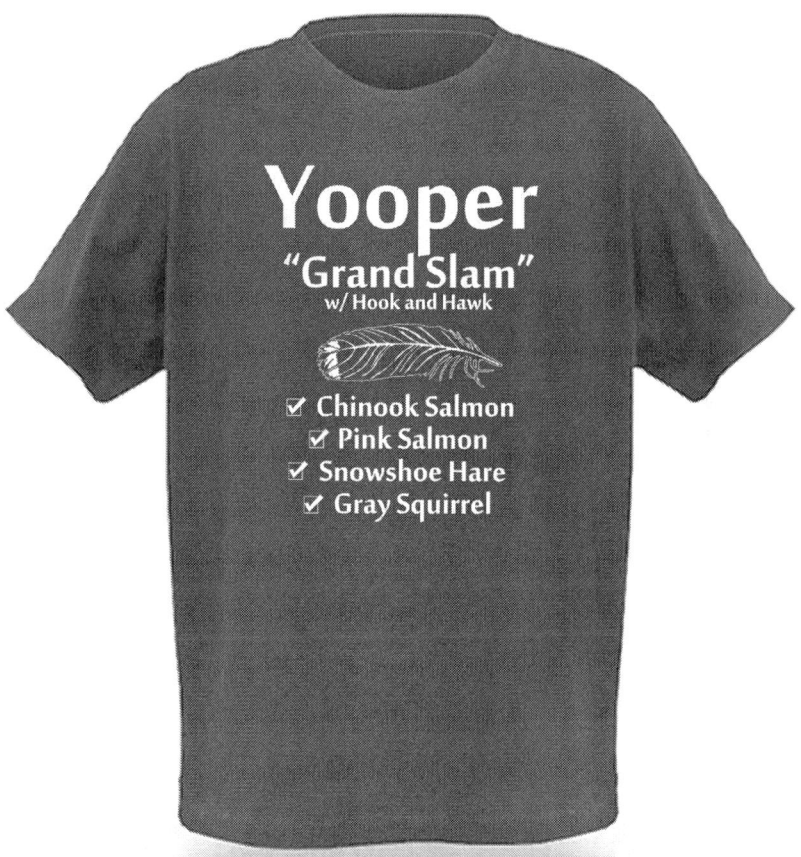

This T-shirt design of a "Hook and Hawk Grand Slam" depicts a passion for falconry and fly fishing for salmon and steelhead. In the fall, a falconer and fly fisherman could catch a pink salmon and chinook salmon with flies, then capture a snowshoe hare and squirrel all in the same day. Now that would be a "grand slam!"

The faces of four of my favorite Harris hawks.

Chapter 25
Why Harris Hawks?

I should not fly Harris hawks in the Eastern Upper Peninsula of Michigan. I can see northern Canada out my window.

It's cold here.

At times it's bitter cold.

In winter the Harris hawks stay in a heated, insulated mew with hockey-rink glass over the barred windows. To my dismay, the cold cuts a chunk out of the hawking season.

Any reasonable falconer living here would fly a red-tail or a goshawk. Both are awesome gamehawks well-suited to this terrain and weather. Red-tailed hawks are best suited to battle our primary quarry — the hard-biting gray squirrels.

But I still fly Harris hawks.

With all the management issues, weather troubles and quarry quandaries, I pondered why.

It's because I remember, I hope and I anticipate.

Call Them Each by Name

I remember standing in my back yard, training my first Harris hawk. She bolted from the glove and I just called her name, "Sarah!" At the sound of her name she swung around and returned without a tidbit. To this day I can recall the feeling of her feet gently landing on my glove.

Recently, in a thick squirrel woods, I flew three hawks — Sadie, Samwise and Gabi — by myself. When any one of them was out of position, I'd simply call his or her name and he or she would fly into a tree above me. If I held up my gauntlet whichever Harris' name I called would come to the glove.

Often I follow their name with a loud "Huup!" It means "Come!" When the terriers hear it they know that I suspect quarry to flush and they come running too.

In an emergency — such as hawks flying toward traffic or a trans- former pot — I blow a Scotland Yard police whistle. Every hawk knows that whistle means "get food now." It's the only time I feed them anything on the fist. The hawks race each other to the glove, which is interesting with three birds in the air and only two hands!

Harris Bolt

Joe Vorro of Lansing, Michigan — the first falconer I ever met — and I were hawking a short grass field in South Bend, Indiana with a female Harris that perched on a shoulder-high bush when a cottontail bolted right under her. She dropped to ground level and bolted after it. Less then 15 feet later it was captured. Vorro, who hunted with a goshawk, was amazed at her burst of speed.

Noises They Make

Sadie whines when she see, a squirrel in a tree or a rabbit sneaking through cover. When I hear that whine, I know something is in mortal danger. Once she located a squirrel 70 yards away in a tall poplar tree at the corner of a red house. The elderly Italian lady fed birds, and squirrels were welcome visitors to her bird feeders. We are also wel- come to chase the squirrels on her property. As I approached the tree I wondered if the squirrel had already escaped until I heard her whine.

Moments later she bolted after the climber which barely eluded her talons as it darted around the trunk and through a crotch then scram- bled toward the top of the leafless tree. So Sadie and Sam found it again and each took shots at it. As it avoided the cast's attacks, it ran down the trunk while wrapping around the trunk as it descended. Sadie stooped after it and somehow corkscrewed around the trunk, snatching the biter off it.

As they fell 25 feet to the ground, Sadie kept repositioning her feet as the squirrel tried to bite her. When they hit the ground, I dived in to assist.

I was not needed.

Hawk Mentors

Intermewed Harris hawks become mentors for young hawks. In late summer and early fall I often fly an adult hawk whose weight is too high. She is so fat that she won't return to the glove — even for food. But when quarry was flushed she charged after it and often grabbed it from underneath the feet of the young birds. When the hunt was over, we simply walked toward the vehicle and the adult bird was sitting on it awaiting her ride home. She did not want us to go home without her.

Our favorite quarry, a black-tailed jackrabbit, mocks us by sitting in the open while looking at its friend the barbed-wire fence in Kansas.

Born to Catch Jackrabbits

The huge Kansas pasture slowly sloped down toward a dry creek bed, then climbed to towering heights to the east. Sadie perched in a tall tree at a John Deere dealership some 60 yards west of the field. The other four Harris hawks were riding on gloves. Sadie prefers trees.

She was out of position when the jack bolted in front of our group. After it escaped the group of hawks a moan rose from the crowd. Then we realized the flight was not over. Sadie was still pursuing it.

She flew with intent. Somehow she thought she could catch it.

The Michigan jackrabbit hawking crew pose in front of the Dodge City, Kansas sign in October 2010, from left: Scott McKamey (holding "Gabi"), Chris Shaw (with "Mia"), Greg Agoston, John Shuell (with "Marie"), and Jared Shaw.

More than 217 yards (according to measurements from Google Maps) from her tree, she closed the gap on it and threw out the landing gear for a catch. The wily rabbit darted sharply to the left and deftly avoided Sadie as it had the other Harris hawks.

Coming down the opposite slope, Sadie was in a tree by the creek, when we bumped a jackrabbit toward her. The other hawks left the gloves and turned the jack, which she promptly slammed into from the other direction. It broke free, but the incident made Sadie more determined to catch jacks.

We flushed a jack in a pasture and Sadie flew it down in 20 yards. As she reached for it, the jack cut hard to the left and made a tight 360-degree circle around her. She stalled out and hit the ground as the rabbit kept running east. Gabi and John Shuell's Marie flew over Sadie. Their pursuit motivated her to keep chasing. She flew past the other hawks and slammed into the black-tail. Chris Shaw's Mia, who flew in from the south, assisted with the cantankerous critter.

Early one morning as we were climbing over a pasture fence, we flushed a jackrabbit. It ran. Three hawks chased it, but the jack disappeared into some tall grass. Sadie perched on the slanted bank of the roadside. On her low perch, she could not see the jack when we reflushed it moments later. Hearing "Ho, ho, ho," she flew upward over the fence and bolted after the quarry. A teenager and I ran after her. At the last moment the jack darted left toward the nearby fence. Sadie grabbed it and was pulled into the barbs. Moments later I saw Sadie hung on the barbed wire by her neck and left wing. Under her was a black-tail with both her feet planted firmly on its face. Fortunately, she was not punchered. The same could not be said of the rabbit.

After her first jackrabbit trip, Sadie was a different hawk. She chased everything with an abundance of confidence, courage, excitement and success. It seemed like she was born to hawk jackrabbits and finding her calling set her free to excel at every quarry.

Flight of Fancy

Late one fall, I hunted the behind my parents' home in North Branch, Michigan. From their backyard we could see across the treeless feral field all the way to a parallel road to the west. Less than 20 yards from the house, we flushed a pheasant that roared off toward the west.

By reflex Sarah bolted from the glove at the rooster. She was too late. The pheasant flushed too early and too far out for her to have a chance. But she chased. Her wingbeats acknowledged her ambition — her flight of fancy.

As the rooster flew, it kept increasing its lead.

Sarah kept flying, but not all out. She simply kept rowing in the mild wind.

The pheasant was hundreds of yards away from me as its gap grew over Sarah.

Then within a 100 yards of the road, the rooster set its wings, glided a little, then flapped again. Instantly Sarah's wingbeat quickened. The pheasant glided again as it flew over the road. Sarah's pace was furious.

As the rooster dropped into the brush line, the black hawk plunged in after it.

And caught it.

Google Maps measurements indicated the flight was more than 600 yards.

Her flight of fancy became a pleasant pheasant flight.

Surprise Duck

While hawking a country wood lot, Sadie flew out of a pine tree to smash a duck in sheet-water in a harvested cornfield. She caught it, and sat in the foot-deep water with the duck in her feet. However, she had a confused look on her face as she wondered where the duck had gone. Moments later the mallard popped up through Sadie's tail and flew off.

Sadie sat there for a few minutes while trying to access the situation which apparently worked as later ducks were not so fortunate.

Upwind Jackrabbit

At one NAFA Meet, our group of eight decided to hold our Harris hawks on the glove while we walked upwind to hunt with the wind at our backs.

"Hang on to your hawk even if a jack flushes," our leader said. "Don't let them go. It will only waste time."

Well, you know where this story is going.

As we walked, I enjoyed a casual conversation with an eastern falconer. I got distracted and was not even looking forward when the black-tail took off. Instantly Sarah bated.

She was off before I could close my glove around her jesses.

The leader moaned.

I was the only disobedient one. But not willfully.

"I'm sorry," I said sincerely, as Sarah flew over the sage brush still chasing the rabbit.

"She'll never catch it in this wind," a voice announced as I watched her wingbeats.

"She thinks she has a shot," I rebutted. Experience had shown she knew better than me if she could catch fleeing quarry.

I started running.

Soon she pitched up and rolled into a pumping stoop into the waist-high sage.

Immediately the black-tailed jackrabbit leaped high enough for all to see that Sarah was attached to it.

The jack belched out a deep growl.

It was his last.

Cooperative Flights

The organized chaos and the beauty of Harris hawk cooperation always intrigued me.

One cold winter day with six new inches of snow, I took Sadie, Sam and Gabi squirrel hawking near a local gravel pit. After a few unsuccessful flights at gray biters, the hawks spotted a black squirrel. For more than 15 minutes of non-stop action, they chased it from one heavily-branched pine tree to the next. When each of them struck at

Chris Shaw, of Eagle, Michigan, with his 2008 female Harris hawk, Mia and a black-tailed jackrabbit caught near Dodge City, Kansas.

the squirrel — and became entangled in the snarl of branches — a second would stoop as it scampered to the next tree. When it eluded the second, the third attacked. Then the cycle repeated.

And repeated.

Finally, they pressed the black beast hard enough that it ran down a fallen tree. The pine tree rested at a 45-degree angle against the squirrel's last place of refuge. As it ran down the top of the fallen tree, Sadie attacked. As her yellow foot reached out to grab it, the climber simply darted around the trunk and without losing any speed ran down the underside of the tree. As Gabi slammed into the snow bank piled at the roots of the pine, the black one disappeared into the white shelter.

Sam and Sadie sat breathless in the nearby trees as Gabi stared in disbelief at the snow bank.

After scanning the fresh snow signs of the quarry's escape, I realized it had not. It was holed up in the snow cover roots of two trees.

So I dug.

For 15 minutes I kept digging in the snow. Eventually, Gabi flew into a tree.

Finally, I realized the squirrel had slipped away.

In frustration, I slammed the roots one more time with my beating stick.

As instantly as it had disappeared into the snow, the black beast shot out of it and charged up 45-degree tree.

All three hawks simultaneously attacked it on the climb. All the trio crashed into the tree as the squirrel reached the thick branches.

The hawks were all caught up, but the squirrel was not.

Depicted above is the cast of characters of the "A Windy Jack" story. The background image is the field where the adventure took place.

A Windy Jack

On the last day of a Kansas jackrabbit hawking trip our group of

Michigan falconers faced the daunting task of hawking in 25-plus mph winds.

It was all but hopeless.

But it was our last day, so were weren't spending it in the motel.

We flew four female Harris hawks — Sadie, Gabi, Marie and Mia — in a field near the city airport.

Many jackrabbits flushed in the field, and all knew how to use the gale against us. Constantly we would hawk downwind, then circle around back upwind to make another downwind sweep. Six of us formed a line to work a small draw with some short cover the jackrabbits use. About halfway down the shallow draw, a jack shot out from the cover 10 yards from us. All four hawks were upwind and excitedly pursued it. What followed was a massive whirl of black and russet wings striking at a brown blur that zipped and zagged around to elude the darkness.

After it dodged the first hawk, it turned upwind only to find one of the other birds was attacking it from that direction. That hawk — which one no one knew — turned the rabbit back downwind, where it was promptly attacked by another, which turned it again. At every opportunity the rabbit would turn back into the wind. Each time one of the four hawks would be coming from upwind.

We could do nothing but watch the small black tornado whirling around a scampering brown tumbleweed.

On one of the jack's attempts to run upwind, one of the hawks finally put a foot on him. He shot straight up as she tried to get her other foot on the quarry. Before any of the other trio could assist her, they hit the ground and the jackrabbit was running again.

The strike by the hawk spurred the rest to intensify their efforts. One turned the jack again, a second took a swipe at it, then Mia slammed into it.

"Mia caught it," Chris Shaw said, "But she would have never caught it without the help of the other three."

A perfect example of cooperative Harris hawks.

A Cast of Hawks, Over a Brace of Terriers

One late February afternoon we visited the home of my sponsor, Mike Jones, from South Bend. After five months of flying the cast of Harris hawks and a brace of terriers were in excellent form and performed like a Navy SEALs unit. I wanted my former sponsor to see their teamwork. The unit included Prince, my rat terrier from a German immigrant's farm, and a terrier-poodle-Chihuahua mix named Missy. A church member named her and gave her to me because the ugly, 11-pound mutt was "killing her cats."

The afternoon weather was cold and windy and great rabbit fields were only five miles away, but Mike was reluctant to venture there. I asked if he had any rabbits in that tall brush along a drainage ditch behind his house. He said there were but they'd be impossible to catch, because if they come out of the cover at all they would be back in it within three feet.

I convinced him to give a try anyway just to see how the dogs and hawks worked. Within minutes the dogs flushed two cottontails. As Mike had said, they returned to the thick, head-high cover within a yard. But the terriers reflushed them.

Some 12 minutes later, each hawk had caught a rabbit.

Even Mike — a longtime goshawk man — expressed his amazement.

Yes, I fly Harris hawks because:
I remember,
I hope,
I anticipate seeing it. . .
. . . again next season.

Some people think they were born to be falconers. I know I was born to preach the Gospel of Jesus and fly Harris hawks.

A Favorite Falconry Quote

Toby Bradshaw:

"Shadow" employs one attack style almost exclusively, uncomplicated but effective — a full-afterburner, deep-wing-beat pursuit ending with a crunch into the sagebrush sounding like an anvil thrown into a tub of corn flakes.

From "Shoals of Jackrabbits in the Sagebrush Ocean"
September 2005, Page 9.
At http://home.comcast.net/~baywingdb

Appendix I

Previously Published Articles

- Young Love: Sarah's First Season. *Hawk Chalk,* April 1984
- Raider of the Lost Squirrel. *NAFA Journal,* 1983
- "Patty" the West Nile Virus Bald Eagle. *The Sault Evening News,* (from multiple articles 2002 to 2009)
- A Cast of Harris Hawks. *NAFA Journal,* 1984
- Fence Jumping. *NAFA Journal,* 1989
- Hawking Lamar Jacks — Harris-Style. *Hawk Chalk,* April 1985
- Rescuing a Jackrabbit. *Bond with the Wild,* October 1993
- Khan of the Sky. *NAFA Journal,* 1987
- The Falconer's Psalm. *NAFA Journal,* 1981
- A Coach's Delight. *NAFA Journal,* 1988
- The Pit. *The Wittenburg Door,* April/May, 1987
- Hawking at the 1986 NAFA Meet. *Hawk Chalk,* April 1987
- Dialogue 101. *Hoosier Hawker,* 1987
- Sarah Kedar — A Memorial & Sonnet to a Lost Love. *NAFA Journal,* 1986
- Removable Anklets. *Hawk Chalk,* August 1982
- Fishing the Sky: Hawk Banding at Whitefish Point. *The Sault Evening News,* (from multiple articles 2002 to 2010)
- Hoodwinking. *NAFA Journal,* 1990
- On Eagles Wings, Isaiah 40:31. *Christian Standard,* November 3, 1985 (reprinted in many magazines)
- Animal Rights — Christian Morals. *Christian Standard,* July 22, 1990 (reprinted in several magazines)
- Fine Day for Squirrels. *Kindle eBooks,* December 26, 2009.

All about the Birds

Matthew 10:29 (NIV)

Jesus said, "Are not two sparrows sold for a penny? Yet not one of them will fall to the ground outside your Father's care."

Kenn Filkins:

If God cares for the sparrows, how much more so does He care for hawks, falcons, eagles and you?

Matthew 6:25-26 (NASB)

Jesus said, "I say to you, do not be worried about your life, as to what you will eat or what you will drink; nor for your body, as to what you will put on. Is not life more than food, and the body more than clothing?

"Look at the birds of the air, that they do not sow, nor reap nor gather into barns, and yet your heavenly Father feeds them. Are you not worth much more than they?

"And who of you by being worried can add a single hour to his life?"

Appendix II
The Parable of the Pit
By Kenn Filkins

A man fell into a pit and couldn't get himself out.

A subjective person came along and said, "I *feel* for you down there."

An objective person came along and said, "It's logical that someone would fall down into that pit."

A Pharisee said, "Only bad people fall into a pit."

Confucius said, "If you would have listened to me, you wouldn't be in that pit."

Buddha said, "Your pit is only a state of mind."

A realist said, "Now that's a pit!"

A scientist calculated the pressure necessary, pounds per square inch, to get him out of the pit.

A geologist told him to appreciate the rock strata in the pit.

An evolutionist said, "You will die in the pit so you can't produce any more pit-falling offspring."

The country inspector asked, "Did you have a permit to dig that pit?"

A professor gave him a lecture on "The Elementary Principles of the Pit."

A self-pitying person said, "You haven't seen anything until you've seen my pit!"

An optimist said, "Things could be worse."

A pessimist said, "Things *will* get worse."

But Jesus saw the man in the pit, took him by the hand, and lifted him out.

First published in *The Wittenburg Door.* April/May, 1987.

About the Author

Kenn Filkins, of Sault Ste. Marie, Michigan, has written eight books, and edited — and wrote for — the award-winning hardcover book, *Bond with the Wild: A Celebration of American Falconry.* His other books include: *Comfort Those Who Mourn: How to Preach Personalized Funeral Messages, A Comforting Word, Fly Fishing for Salmon & Steelhead of the Great Lakes, Characters of Calvary, Seven Sayings One Friday, Personalized Funerals in the Digital Age,* and *Seven Saying: The Impact of Jesus' Words from the Cross* (a Kindle eBook).

Kenn as been a preacher for over 30 years, serving churches in Indiana, Iowa and Michigan. He is in his tenth year of pulpit ministry at the Donaldson Church in the Sault. Filkins graduated with honors from Great Lakes Christian College in 1979, where he won the "Dracma Award" for Biblical language studies.

For 11 years, he has been the editor of the daily newspaper for the eastern third of the Upper Peninsula of Michigan. He is currently the editor of the North American Falconers' Association's *Hawk Chalk,* a tri-annual publication. He has written hundreds of magazine articles on hunting, fishing, falconry and a wide variety of Christian topics. He has won writing and photography awards. Kenn and his wife, Marti, own a high-tech, action photography business.

Contact the Author

For information on other books by Kenn Filkins or for details about falconry, contact the author in the following ways:

• Email: kennf@charter.net

• Phone: 906-440-4921

• Website: www.filkinsfoto.com

• US Mail: Kenn Filkins
             533 Maple St.
             Sault Ste. Marie, MI 49783

7581374R0

Made in the USA
Charleston, SC
20 March 2011